BILL BREMNER

FIFTY DEFINING FIXTURES

Dave Tomlinson

AMBERLEY

For Adele, with all my love.

First published 2017

Amberley Publishing
The Hill, Stroud
Gloucestershire, GL5 4EP

www.amberley-books.com

British Library Cataloguing in Publication Data.
A catalogue record for this book is available from the British Library.

ISBN 978 1 4456 5241 2 (print)
ISBN 978 1 4456 7033 1 (ebook)

Origination by Amberley Publishing.
Printed in the UK.

Contents

Introduction

What ... set him apart from other great players, was his fierce desire to be out there and his will to win. He'd have stitches in a gashed leg, or a swollen ankle, and you'd think, 'Billy won't be fit.' But sure enough, he'd be there, leading us out with this wonderful 'We can't be beaten' attitude.

Peter Lorimer

I had the honour and pleasure of seeing Billy Bremner play in the flesh, in his prime, as I caught the Leeds United bug at nine years old – there's only a dim memory of the 1960s, the first championship and *that* clash with Dave Mackay, but I was there when the Whites faced treble disappointments in 1970, the season when Bremner was elected Footballer of the Year.

A stereotypical Scot with his red hair, jutted-out chin and a fierce will to win, Bremner could start an argument in a telephone box; small in stature he might have been but Bremner was a colossus among footballers, fearless, fearsome and ferocious. He took no prisoners on the pitch, but was the life and soul off it. He might have been a nasty little piece of work, but he was our nasty little piece of work!

The Leeds fans loved wee Billy, and the club named him their greatest player of all time in 2000. A statue of Bremner in characteristic arms-aloft pose fronts the club shop at Elland Road, a symbolic shrine and gathering place for supporters of a club with which he is synonymous.

Bremner epitomised the best days of both Leeds United and Scotland: Elland Road's golden years under Don Revie and the afternoon when Scotland slugged it out with Brazil in the 1974 World Cup finals – halcyon days when football was a man's game, you lived by the sword, died by the sword and enjoyed a beer after the game with opponents you had spent ninety minutes kicking the life out of on the pitch.

Bremner excited the passions – the good, the bad and the ugly – of football followers, an irritating wasp of a player who never gave an opponent a moment's peace, and one of the most gifted and exquisite players of his generation.

William John Bremner was born on 9 December 1942 in Stirling, representing Scotland at schoolboy level.

After signing for Leeds in 1959, Bremner spent seventeen years at Elland Road, leading the club to many honours and representing Scotland on more than fifty occasions. He scored 114 goals in 773 first team appearances, including 587 in the Football League, before winding down his playing career with Hull. As manager, Bremner led Doncaster to promotion from the Fourth Division in 1981 and repeated the feat three years later.

Bremner was appointed manager of his beloved Leeds, then in the Second Division, in 1985. He took them to the FA Cup semi-finals and the verge of promotion in 1987, but was sacked a year later.

He died of a heart attack on 7 December 1997.

When Billy Bremner took us across the white line, whether it was at Elland Road or Anfield or Old Trafford, Stamford Bridge, those players, my team, we died for Leeds United, we died for that club ... Billy was the best player who ever played, they don't make players like him today.

Allan Clarke

Chelsea 1-3 Leeds United
First Division
23 January 1960

Bill Lambton had negligible impact in a short, uncelebrated spell as manager of Leeds United, but he had the foresight (or fortune) to sign both Don Revie and Billy Bremner, irrevocably changing the club's destiny.

When Lambton and chairman Harry Reynolds travelled north to try and sign Scottish Schoolboys star Bremner, there was a major weakness in their game plan: the youngster knew nothing about United, asking boyhood pal Tommy Henderson, who was signed at the same time: 'Who the hell are they? Are they in the Fourth Division or something?' Henderson reassured Bremner that Leeds were a Division One club, albeit a struggling one. Leeds were not Billy's first choice:

As well as Arsenal and Chelsea, there was interest from Sheffield Wednesday and Aston Villa. It was quite flattering. The truth is that I really wanted to join Celtic and I was hoping that they would make a firm bid before the others did. My father had other ideas. He told me quite plainly that he was not going to have me get caught up with any religious controversy – and that automatically ruled out Celtic because of the sectarianism between them and Rangers. 'You're going to England and that's that.' I could never argue with my father ... he would always have the last word.

The two lads were stricken by homesickness and it wasn't long before Henderson returned north; selection for United reserves against Preston was enough to persuade Bremner to commit for another year. Bremner said:

I kept setting myself what I believed were impossible targets and saying that if I didn't achieve those targets then I would go home ... I never thought I would make the reserves by the age of 16 but I did. I never believed I'd be in the first team at 17, but sure enough I managed it. It came to a point where I simply couldn't go home.

I had a couple of conversations with Jack Taylor [Lambton's successor] ... I told him that I felt I should have broken into the first team by now, I was consistently performing well for the reserves, yet for whatever reason it hadn't happened for me ... I told him I was thinking about getting myself a move back to Scotland ... He listened to me and understood my frustration. His parting advice was that it would be in my best interests not to seek a move away from Leeds but to stick it out, as bigger things awaited me while he was manager.

Bremner remained unsettled, but at the end of January 1960 Taylor gave Billy his first team debut away to Chelsea, selected at outside-right with Don Revie inside him.

England international Revie, Footballer of the Year in 1955 and architect of the Revie Plan, had come to national prominence with Manchester City, before unexpectedly joining Leeds in November 1958.

Despite beating West Ham 3-0 the previous weekend, Leeds were eighteenth, four points above the relegation places, far from ideal circumstances in which to debut.

The experienced Revie took Bremner under his wing, doing everything in his power to settle him in, forging a bond that would keep them joined at the hip for twenty years.

It was Revie who told Bremner that he was to make his debut. 'He saw me in the car park and gave me the news. Chris Crowe was doing National Service and had to play for the Army.'

Revie arranged for them to share a room in the London hotel where the players stayed before the game, seeing to it that Bremner was in bed by 10 p.m. and rose at 7 a.m. the next morning to accompany him on a long walk.

When the game commenced, Revie made sure Bremner got an early touch to settle his nerves: 'I could see from the start that Billy had the ability to go right to the top. I wanted to see if he would use that ability. I didn't need to worry. He had no trouble with the big-time atmosphere, he was confident, even cheeky, in that first debut game.'

Phil Brown reported in the *Yorkshire Evening Post*: 'His was no sensational debut with the miry pitch and rain all being against a lightweight youth shining. But all the main football qualities were there – enthusiasm, guts, intelligence, most accurate use of the ball and unselfishness.'

The game went well, with Leeds winning 3-1 thanks to a brace from John McCole and a goal from Noel Peyton. Bremner recalled later:

Before the kick-off I looked around and could see famous faces everywhere. Once the game started, though, I forgot about that, and it was not until it was all over that I once again took in the fact that I had been playing football in the First Division surrounded by internationals.

I was delighted with that win at Chelsea for more than one reason. Not only was it a brilliant start to my career to be on the winning side but I had also had a reasonable game, which, I thought, might earn me at least another chance in the first team. It was also a bit of a response to Chelsea who, I had discovered, like Arsenal, had not come back to me after the trials because they'd considered me to be too small to make a professional footballer.

It's difficult to know what to think when you make your first team debut; the pitch was dreadful. I thought other teams would be as professional as we were, but instead I found that Chelsea would stoop to any level to intimidate and bully. It riled me and ensured that I was all the more determined to get one over on them.

All I wanted at the start was to get my first touch of the ball out of the way. Fortunately this happened fairly quickly and when I laid a pass on to Don Revie, I immediately settled down into my game. Wilbur Cush constantly reminded me to ignore abusive and foul comments made by the Chelsea players and their crowd. He reminded me that the abuse should be taken as a back-handed compliment, as it meant they saw me as a threat and that I was playing well. By the end of the game I was being nasty to the Chelsea players who had been having a go at me and they didn't like it one bit!

Bremner was to clash swords with Chelsea on many occasions and they would always rue rejecting him. Too small? Take that!

The career of Billy Bremner was on the move!

Stamford Bridge
Attendance: 18,963

Chelsea: Matthews, P. Sillett, J. Sillett, Crowther, Scott, Anderton, Brabrook, Brooks, Livesey, Greaves, Blunstone.

Leeds United: Wood, Ashall, Hair, Cush, Charlton, Gibson, Bremner, Revie, McCole, Peyton, Meek.

Leeds United 4-3 Manchester City
First Division
19 March 1960

Bremner did enough on his debut to retain his place for the following game, a fortnight later against West Bromwich Albion, but United lost 4-1 and the Scot gave way to Chris Crowe.

Jack Taylor had been sufficiently impressed, though, to cash in on one of his few marketable assets, and he sold Crowe to Blackburn for £25,000 a couple of weeks later, and Bremner became a fixture in the side.

His third game saw Leeds crash at home to Blackpool, dropping them into the relegation zone, but four days later they faced Birmingham, the side immediately above them, at Elland Road.

Don Revie gave United a 2-0 lead inside thirty-four minutes. The Blues pulled one back just before the interval, but Bremner opened his scoring account for United after seventy-three minutes to restore a two-goal cushion. Leeds were a brittle side, however, and Birmingham stormed back to equalise with two goals inside the next six minutes. There were only 8,557 spectators to witness the 3-3 draw, which left United anchored in the bottom two.

They were not ready to surrender, though, and on 19 March welcomed Manchester City, another struggling side.

The crowd was swollen to 32,545 by the chance to witness the City debut of Denis Law, recently signed from Huddersfield.

The report in *The Times* concentrated on Law:

A fair-haired young man, frail in appearance, but of whiplash quality, he himself seemed the least conscious of the golden yoke, valued at some £53,000, around his slender neck. A fading fortune to revive, a duty to be done in a game which he patently loves, he set out with a firm step under his new banner. Yet in spite of his hypnotic appearance Leeds won desperately at the very last breath and some 35,000 Yorkshiremen breathed a sigh as their team, for the moment at least, took a step towards the light.

That it needed two penalty kicks by McCole in the final stages to turn apparent defeat into sudden victory merely added to the tension, though in neither case did any real stigma remain with Manchester. They were the sort of things that often happen in a match of this character where nerves twang and where gentlemanly thud follows human blunder. Yet justice was finally done in a roundabout way, even if the first of those penalties – making it 3-3 – surprised even the mildest of Yorkshiremen, for in the last analysis it was the goalkeeping of Trautmann ... which for so long supported the attacking touches of Law caught in the ebb and flow of an untidy battle.

In the opening half Law must have doubted whether he had stepped up into the supposedly higher grade of the Championship, so inaccurate and hesitant was the general pattern. Both sides struggled with the neurosis of survival as first Revie with a sharp pass sent Peyton in to put Leeds ahead, only to see the lead quickly squandered, as Gibson, with a blind disregard, pushed the ball past his own goalkeeper at the other end. Next Bremner, a 17-year-old winger of some promise, sent Leeds clear a second time through a scattered defence with a shot in off the far post, but almost immediately, at the 25th minute, Law began to make his presence felt.

Manchester, indeed, now seemed to be heading for their first away win since December 15. A colonnade of tributes began to be prepared for Law when suddenly the tide turned. Revie, slower than of old but still sophisticated of touch, inspired a storming Yorkshire revival. Supported by the strength of his full-backs and Goodwin, a new colleague from Old Trafford in the rear, and by the liveliness of little Bremner at his side, Revie mounted the last counter challenge against a tottering, yawning defence.

At the kick-off the massed flight of photographers, amid mock boos and cheers, had settled like vultures around the Leeds goal. Now Law produced something for them to embalm on film and plate. Flicking a pass to Hayes and sidestepping Gibson, he took the return in his stride, beat Ashall's tackle, and flashed in a fine goal to make it 2-2. More and more now he became the puppet master. But the cultured Barnes apart, few of the figures around him answered his touches promptly until at last, 20 minutes after the interval, another proficient pass from him sent Barlow in to put City 3-2 ahead.

Trautmann made superb saves from Revie himself and McCole, both at point blank range, then from Bremner: when he was beaten, Branagan and Sear cleared off the Manchester goal line. But with 10 minutes left came the twist. McCole and Branagan both stumbled over the ball harmlessly. A penalty was awarded mysteriously. McCole drove it home and then repeated the dose in the dying seconds when Oakes impulsively handled Bremner's centre. Leeds were home and Law, Barnes, and Trautmann, their efforts wasted, became figures of dejection.

Law commented:

Billy was like a little demon. He was everywhere all at the same time. I was a young lad myself and he certainly impressed me. I think everyone thought that his energy came from the excitement of youth, but he always played like that until the day he retired. We thought we had done enough to win that day but Leeds just got the edge and beat us. Billy shook hands with me afterwards and we congratulated each other on scoring.

The result saw Leeds move above Birmingham and out of the relegation places, but they could not maintain the revival and won just three further games, dooming them to relegation.

Bremner was distraught at the outcome and remained homesick, constantly agitating for a move back to his homeland. He was forced to tread water for the next couple of years as United wallowed without direction in a sea of mediocrity.

Elland Road
Attendance: 32,545

Leeds United: Burgin, Ashall, Hair, Gibson, Charlton, Goodwin, Bremner, Revie, McCole, Peyton, Meek

Manchester City: Trautmann, Branagan, Sear, Barnes, McTavish, Oakes, Barlow, Law, McAdams, Hayes, Colbridge

Leeds United 2-0 Swansea Town
Second Division
10 March 1962

In March 1961, Don Revie was a surprise appointment as player-manager after the Board accepted the resignation of Jack Taylor towards the end of a poor season.

The winter that followed was a desperate one as Revie's brave new world seemed set to collapse after poor form in the autumn. Revie, building for the future with a hugely promising youth development programme, was forced to contend in the here and now with the very real threat of relegation to Division Three.

November and December brought some relief as Leeds beat Middlesbrough and Walsall, then saw off prospective champions Liverpool on 23 December, with Billy Bremner scoring the only goal. However, amid those successes came a defeat at bottom club Charlton and victories were rare after the Liverpool triumph. A home reverse to Plymouth on 24 February saw Leeds slump to the foot of the table, in danger of an unprecedented plunge into Division Three.

The club's financial standing was precarious but the directors' generosity offered a lifeline. Revie had already been given the money to recruit former Manchester City teammate Billy McAdams, but March's transfer deadline was looming and Revie had to act swiftly. Clutching a transfer kitty, the manager set off in pursuit of six signings; he returned with three newcomers.

The first was Burnley reserve Ian Lawson, for whom the Turf Moor club demanded an exorbitant £20,000. Goalscoring was United's major shortcoming and Revie reasoned that it was a worthwhile gamble.

Lawson made his debut on 3 March in the Yorkshire derby at Huddersfield, partnering Jack Charlton up front. Revie recalled himself for his first game since September and Charlton got on the scoresheet, but Leeds went down 2-1, their third successive defeat. The only glimmer of hope was that relegation rivals Brighton, Bristol Rovers and Charlton all lost.

The match marked the end for Revie as a player, though he had not seen that many summers more than his immediate replacement.

United paid £10,000 to sign experienced left-back Cliff Mason from Sheffield United but it was his other signing who made the lasting impression. On 9 March, *The Times* reported the transfer in muted terms: 'R. Collins, the Everton and former Scotland and Celtic inside forward, was transferred to Leeds United last night. The fee [£25,000] was the highest paid by Leeds, and the highest received by Everton.' It was a terse record of a move that transformed the history of Leeds United.

Many critics were astonished that the club's future had been staked on a thirty-one-year-old who stood just 5 feet 4 inches tall, and seemed to have his best days behind him.

Collins was one of the most inspirational of post-war inside forwards, making his name with Celtic before joining Everton in 1959. The Merseysiders were rebuilding and the chance to recover their initial outlay was too much to resist.

Collins wore Revie's number eight shirt for the first time on 10 March against Swansea, among Leeds' closest relegation rivals. Mason and Lawson also featured, while McAdams was recalled with Charlton banished to the reserves.

Bremner had always idolised Collins and it was like a dream come true to share a dressing room with him.

> What a player Bobby was. I used to love to go and watch him. I suppose I could relate closely to him because he was a little guy like me. When I used to see him when I was a lad, he was doing all that I had dreamed of. He was wearing the Celtic shirt and he was capped by Scotland … He controlled the game from midfield. I thought he was fantastic and if I ever wanted to be someone else it would have been Bobby Collins.
>
> He was the best professional I have ever known. He was thirty-one when he joined us and everyone else was writing him off, but he stayed for several years and he played at the top of his game throughout. Even when he was seriously injured he came bouncing back to lead us to new heights. All the young players who were around at the time owed Bobby Collins a big debt for his generalship, his advice and his example.
>
> Whenever he was in the side I felt confident that he would bully, coax, cajole, cool us down whenever we were in danger of losing our heads, encourage and praise us whenever we did anything good, and generally look after us like a father. In the heat of the game he would sense when we were beginning to need a bit of breathing space and he would go into the fight for possession of the ball, plonk a pass upfield for Albert Johanneson to chase, while we at the back breathed a little less hard and pulled ourselves together.
>
> When Bobby went out to play, nothing could put him off his game. He left all his cares behind him in the dressing room and, for the next ninety minutes, only one thing mattered – that everyone should be pulling his guts out for the whole of the game in a tremendous team effort.
>
> I learned many great lessons from Bobby Collins, not the least being able to take the knocks as well as hand them out, and always play the game as a man. They say that one man does not make a team, but Bobby Collins came nearer to doing it than anyone else that I have ever seen on a football field.

Leeds' defeat at Huddersfield, coupled with a Charlton victory three days later, left them sitting adrift, two points below the pack.

Even for a player as resolute and determined as Collins, this was a daunting prospect, but he rose to the challenge with spirit.

The changing of the guard brought instant reward – the Swansea game drew a crowd of 17,314, the third best of the season and more than double the attendance for the Plymouth defeat a fortnight earlier.

Collins enjoyed a dream debut. He opened the scoring, and offered clear evidence that he had lost none of his fire; but it was his intelligence and knowledge of the game that really marked him out as United's saviour, telling the other players where to go and what to do. McAdams added a second to complete a 2-0 victory, United's first in seven matches, which edged them off the bottom on goal average, at the same time dragging Swansea into the relegation dogfight.

It was a crucial result and, though Leeds lost 4-1 the following week at Southampton, set the team up for a crucial unbeaten run.

They battled manfully through their remaining fixtures, building on a stout defence. Just four goals were conceded in eight matches following the Southampton reverse. Yet, for all the fortitude, Leeds still had much to do. As the season entered its final day, they took a testing trip to Newcastle with a point still required to make them safe.

Elland Road
Attendance: 17,314

Leeds United: Younger, Hair, Mason, Cameron, Goodwin, Smith, Bremner, Collins, McAdams, Lawson, Hawksby

Swansea Town: King, Purcell, Sanders, Johnson, Nurse, H. J. Williams, B. D. Jones, E. R. Davies, Webster, Donnelly, J. H. Griffiths

Newcastle United 0-3 Leeds United
Second Division
28 April 1962

Billy Bremner's eleven goals from thirty-nine appearances made him the leading scorer in United's pitiful 1961/62 campaign, prompting a desperate Don Revie to experiment with Jack Charlton up front, but he was no John Charles and a late escape route was fashioned by dour defensive football rather than any sudden rush of goals.

An eight-game unbeaten run, comprising two narrow home victories and six draws, three of them goalless, left United needing a final day draw to keep them up.

The players were understandably nervous as they travelled to Newcastle, though Bobby Collins saw to it that they were focused on getting the right outcome, as recalled by Bremner: 'He never gave us a minute, because he was always telling us to do this, and do that, and do something else, and go tight there, and give it plenty of room in another place, and then get everybody running and running.'

Collins had seen to it that Revie's game plan was followed without question. He introduced a new urgency, demanding that United become the most difficult of teams to beat, saying later:

> He wanted me to instil in the players a never-say-die attitude throughout a game. The defence had to tighten up and be disciplined at the back. I sat in the middle of the park, leaving four in attack, with the wingers coming back to help when necessary.
>
> Don had been trying these tactics without success, but I made my point forcibly to the players that this would be our tactics come what may. Playing as a team was the key to survival. This way we would do no worse than draw, and hopefully snatch a win to avoid relegation.

Bremner was flourishing under Collins' wing, benefiting from the same wisdom and insight previously offered by Revie but now laced with some streetwise cunning. It was a telling combination of gifts, which left an indelible mark on the nineteen-year-old.

The Newcastle match saw United playing into the teeth of a gale, but it was like water off a duck's back as they gave their finest performance for years. Collins was on top of his game and pulled all the strings in midfield, while fleet-footed Albert Johanneson offered a constant outlet.

Not for nothing was the South African winger known as the Black Flash: he had God-given pace and natural skills, including a 'bewitching side step'. When he was bearing down at speed on a back pedalling full-back, unable to fathom which way he was likely to go with his dazzling sleight of foot, he was a wonder to behold. A lithe, subtle footballer with the natural grace of an African athlete, Johanneson was 'blessed with blistering pace, skill on the ball and a terrific shot', according to David Saffer, he 'caused havoc for defences with his dazzling runs and crosses from the left flank.' Johanneson was in peerless form at Newcastle and drove defenders to distraction.

Bremner came close to scoring early on, but for all United's first-half dominance it was thirty-seven minutes before a breakthrough, with Johanneson lashing the ball in off the bar. Billy McAdams hit a post with a header but had better luck in the sixty-fifth minute when he rose to head in after goalkeeper Dave Hollins fumbled Johanneson's cross.

Ten minutes later, Leeds' safety was guaranteed when Bremner's centre was deflected into the net by Newcastle right-back Bobby Keith.

The Magpies did not have the stomach for a fight back and Leeds were not unduly troubled in the closing stages, able to take the trip home to Yorkshire with both the points and their Second Division status safely in the bank. Relegation could have sounded the club's death knell, but the determined football played since Collins' revival offered a glimpse of things to come.

Twenty-seven months on from his first team debut, Billy Bremner was starting to see promise at Elland Road. He still hankered for a move back to his native Scotland but was enjoying playing in a team led by Collins.

St James' Park
Attendance: 21,708

Newcastle United: Hollins, Keith, Clish, Wright, Thompson, Turner, Day, Kerray, Thomas, Allchurch, Fell

Leeds United: Younger, Hair, Mason, Goodwin, Charlton, Smith, Bremner, Collins, McAdams, Bell, Johanneson

Swansea Town 0-2 Leeds United
Second Division
8 September 1962

There was an air of optimism about Elland Road in the summer of 1962: the club's debt had risen to around £150,000 as money was found to support a relegation fight in the spring, and such was the faith in Don Revie that the directors went a step further when they heard the rumours from Italy that a former favourite was on the market. In March, the *Yorkshire Evening Post* carried the headline: 'Now what price John Charles for United?'

Revie's initial strategy had been to attract and nurture the best of the country's teenage talent, but the team's shortcoming had been a distinct shortage of goals, and if Charles could remedy that failing and inspire a promotion push, the directors reasoned, it would be money well spent.

Revie briefed Charles on his ambitions for the club and how central he was to those plans. It was the manager's gifts of persuasion that sealed the Welshman's commitment.

Revie had a knack for getting his man, and used the signing to convince another player that his future lay at Elland Road. Airdrie inside forward Jim Storrie had turned down initial advances the previous season, but when Revie came calling a second time, the Scottish part-timer was convinced.

Revie's game plan was simple – play a pressurising game, denying the opposition space and time, and get the ball forward quickly to Charles. He would secure possession and bring the other forwards into the play, making openings for them to run onto. It sounded effective, but there were flaws.

Firstly, many of the team were into their thirties and ill-equipped for the hard-running game that Revie's plans demanded.

Secondly, Charles had never been an orthodox target man and his time with Juventus had changed him. Italian football demanded a subtle and thoughtful approach, and the guile to avoid being laid low by cynical defenders. Charles retained the physical presence to hold his own against big defenders, but preferred playing to scrapping.

'We were a very physical, hard-working and hard-running side,' explained Storrie. 'It was high-pressure football. We had to put the opposition's players under pressure all over the park ... I was a forward and my first job was to defend. That was the mentality. John was like a duck out of water playing that way. Had he been younger he might have adapted. He wanted to play one-touch football and flick the ball here and there. At the time that wasn't Leeds' style. Long balls were played to the corner flag and John was expected to chase after them. At half-time in one game I remember John saying, "I'm not running my pants off for long balls." And wee Billy Bremner said, "You're making that f***ing obvious!"'

After five games, United were sitting a disappointing eleventh, and questions were being asked about when the star would start to shine.

Nevertheless, a midweek match at home to Bury attracted a crowd of 28,313, the biggest since 1959. After twenty minutes Charles strained his back in a heavy fall, and was rendered a passenger on the wing. Even before the mishap, Leeds were second best, although Billy Bremner opened the scoring in the twenty-sixth minute. Leeds could not retain their lead, and ended up on the wrong end of a 2-1 defeat, which could easily have been heavier.

The fans were hugely disillusioned, and Revie knew as his side dropped into the bottom half of the table that it was simply not good enough.

Storrie, Charles, Freddie Goodwin, Ian Lawson and Willie Bell were all injured, so Revie was down to the bare bones. However, he was so disenchanted with the performance against Bury that he omitted two of his most experienced charges, goalkeeper Tommy Younger and right-back Grenville Hair.

After astutely attracting some of the country's best young talent to Elland Road in the preceding eighteen months, Revie had been nursing them through the lower ranks. The reserve side, which faced Liverpool earlier in the week, had been one of the youngest ever, including seventeen-year-olds Gary Sprake, Paul Reaney, Rodney Johnson and Paul Madeley, Barrie Wright (sixteen), Mike Addy (nineteen), Norman Hunter, Terry Cooper (both eighteen) and Peter Lorimer (fifteen).

Revie had hoped to let them learn their trade in second-string football, but on the Thursday before the game he summoned together Sprake, Reaney, Hunter and Johnson to tell them they were being promoted to the first team.

Billy Bremner had been a fixture in the side for a couple of years, but still knew what it was like to be a boy in a man's world. He would act as the youngsters' older brother and minder.

United were second best in the early exchanges with right winger Jones and centre forward Webster calling Sprake into early action, although both saves were comfortable, helping him to settle.

Things could have been very difficult for Leeds if the 'goal' scored by Webster shortly afterwards had been allowed but he was rightly adjudged offside.

Jack Charlton and Eric Smith began to demonstrate their experience, building confidence in the youngsters, while the pace and energy of youth offered much that had been missing.

Johnson and Hunter were better equipped for Revie's plan than Charles and Goodwin, and Reaney brought verve and pace to the right flank. Indeed, the full-back was in the thick of things early on in ways which would become second nature in the years to come.

Firstly, he linked well with Bremner on an overlap and then he was found covering expertly at the back when Town winger Jones beat Mason and got in a cross. His break forward had been one of the few opportunities that United had for offensive action in the first ten minutes, for Swansea continued to enjoy much of the early possession.

They failed to capitalise, however, and in the eleventh minute it was Leeds who opened the scoring. Johanneson went on one of his characteristic runs down the left, moving the ball inside to Bremner who played Johnson in with a lovely through ball. The debutant had much to do, but he carved his way through a couple of tackles before driving low from an acute angle past goalkeeper Noel Dwyer.

The goal gave the home team pause for thought, allowing Bremner and Collins to gain control of midfield. Along with Peyton, they each came close to adding a second.

Swansea were by no means out of the game and Sprake was in action several times. Indeed, the goalkeeper was one of United's outstanding players, though Leeds had much the better of the first period. Johnson's drive only just beat the bar while Smith fired a powerful shot narrowly wide. All the Leeds forwards had decent games, interchanging and combining cleverly, while Bremner and Collins made sure they provided ample protection and cover to their inexperienced colleagues.

Bremner and Johnson linked well to make a chance for the youngster and then Collins played Johanneson in, although keeper Dwyer saved the day by rushing out to dispossess the South African.

Swansea came out with guns blazing after the break, though Charlton soaked up all they could offer.

Leeds gradually rediscovered their momentum, and were soon 2-0 ahead, following close things for Johanneson and Bremner. Both men were integral when the goal came, and it was a real beauty, described by Phil Brown as 'the best United have scored this season.'

Johanneson began the move, forcing his way up his flank from halfway before feeding Collins. The Scot moved it on into the area for an onrushing Bremner to control, round left-back Griffiths and hammer past the keeper from ten yards.

On the hour, young Johnson was carried off after a heavy collision with the goalkeeper. He had sustained a minor knock minutes earlier, and when he chased in a shot from Hunter he was flattened by the much heavier Dwyer and a stretcher was required. Johnson returned after twelve minutes, but was clearly still suffering the effects of the clash.

The ten men coped admirably in his absence and comfortably held Swansea at bay as the home supporters gave a relentless slow handclap.

According to the *Yorkshire Post*, 'Bremner and Collins provided the best display of inside forward work that United have had for years. United moved faster and played more accurately than at any time this season, or last, the youngsters bringing a zip the side has badly needed.'

It was an impressive new beginning for Leeds United.

Vetch Field
Attendance: 17,696

Swansea Town: Dwyer, B. Hughes, J. H. Griffiths, P Davies, Purcell, Saunders, B. S. Jones, Thomas, Webster, H. J. Williams, Morgans

Leeds United: Sprake, Reaney, Mason, Smith, Charlton, Hunter, Peyton, Bremner, Johnson, Collins, Johanneson

Swansea Town 0-3 Leeds United
Second Division
11 April 1964

Leeds United travelled to face Swansea in April 1964, knowing a point would all but guarantee a return to Division One after four years out of the top flight. While a win was needed to make promotion mathematically certain, their goal average was so superior to third-placed Preston that a draw would be enough.

Don Revie chose to blood nineteen-year-old Terry Cooper in place of Albert Johanneson. Cooper had started his career as an outside-left before being converted by Revie into a full-back; his inclusion promised to make United more solid down the flank, hinting that the manager would be happy to settle for a point.

Cooper had been due to travel as a standby left-back, but Johanneson injured his thigh during training and was left behind.

Revie was confident of victory, if understandably nervous. Swansea were eighteenth, just three points off relegation, but had come close to pulling off a shock before losing 2-1 at Elland Road in November. In addition, they had enjoyed a wonderful cup run, beating First Division Sheffield United and Stoke on the way to a shock victory at champions designate Liverpool.

However, Leeds were battle-hardened, having led the table for most of the season, and they slipped quickly into top gear.

They had no intention of leaving anything to chance and overpowered Swansea, racing into a three-goal lead in little over half an hour. It was Cooper who set the wheels in motion, supplying the cross after fifteen minutes that Alan Peacock slammed home. Within four minutes, Peacock repeated the dose after a corner by Collins was flicked on by Giles.

There was no holding Leeds in this period, although it was another quarter of an hour before they added to their lead. Cooper's corner from the left reached Giles on the edge of the area. He caught the ball perfectly and, although his shot was partially blocked by defender Roy Evans, there was enough pace on the effort for it to find the net. The game was as good as over.

The improvement a 3-0 scoreline brought to United's goal average was too important to risk and Leeds settled for a no-frills performance.

Billy Bremner was still learning how best to fill the central midfield role entrusted to him by Revie following the signing of Giles from Manchester United at the start of the season. He was overshadowed by Collins and the Irish international on the day, but made a solid contribution to a confident and assured performance.

Giles was fully aware of Bremner's qualities from the moment he arrived at Elland Road, saying,

> I could see that Billy had great ability. He was a good distributor, had good close control, great drive and a fine shot on his right side. But like so many of these young players, he had something else too. He was an outstanding character, the most confident player I have ever played with. I never saw him show any nerves in the dressing room before a game. In fact, I'm certain be believed he was going to be the star of every game he played in. And, many times, he was.
>
> Billy and I have vastly different styles of play but we dovetail perfectly. He is capable of overcoming the opposition by sheer physical enthusiasm and reflex action; he dives in for the ball as soon as he sees it. On the other hand, I think I am calmer and more studied in my approach to the game.
>
> While Billy is buzzing about the field, my function is to track him down in order to get him out of trouble if need be and keep feeding him with the bail.
>
> The best way to sum up our partnership is to say that Billy looks for positions from which he can force things to happen while I get into positions from which I can persuade things to happen.
>
> Part of the reason we were so effective, is that we always covered for one another. In fact, I often laugh when I hear them talking these days about the holding role, or the midfielder sitting in front of the defence protecting the back four, even though it is completely impossible for one player to protect the back four. I had a holding role if Billy was going forward, and vice versa, otherwise there was no holding to be done. We weren't trying to hold, we were trying to play. It was all about getting the right balance between us, and by an eerie coincidence, we both ended up scoring exactly 115 goals for Leeds from midfield.

Collins played supremely in an anchor role and, with Giles and Cooper tucking in, gaps proved hard to find, though United's conservative approach allowed Swansea into the game in the second half. When they did manage to carve out an opportunity, they found Gary Sprake the equal of everything they could throw at him.

The comfortable 3-0 victory confirmed United's promotion and with Preston and Sunderland both involved in scoreless draws the result also strengthened the club's title bid. The *Yorkshire Post*'s Eric Stanger:

> Few inside forwards work harder than Collins and generally they are a hard-working race – they have to be in the modern game. Few players can strike such a response from their colleagues. His influence both in the dressing room and on the field has been incalculable. It may be an overstatement to say that he has made Billy Bremner into one of the best wing-halves in the country, but not so much so. Bremner, I know, has such respect and affection for his fellow Scot and his football has improved so much under his lead that United, who could not get £25,000 for him a couple of seasons back, would now not take double that fee for him.
>
> Bremner and Collins have formed the hub round which the team has revolved – the midfield dynamo, as current football phraseology has it. They are responsible for the quick transformation from defence to attack, which is so essential if the modern blanket defence system is not to be completely stultifying.

Leeds United had toiled hard and with scant praise outside the confines of Elland Road all season. They fully merited the chance to let their hair down and took it with gusto. Stage one of the Revie revolution was complete.

Vetch Field
Attendance: 14,321

Swansea Town: Dwyer, R. S. Evans, B. Hughes, Johnson, Purcell, H. J. Williams, Jones, Draper, E. Thomas, MacLaughlin, B. C. Evans

Leeds United: Sprake, Reaney, Bell, Bremner, Charlton, Hunter, Giles, Weston, Peacock, Collins, Cooper

Leeds United 4-2 Liverpool
First Division
26 August 1964

United's acquaintance with the big time kicked off in earnest on Wednesday 26 August 1964. Their first game the previous Saturday had brought victory at Aston Villa, but the midlanders were limited opponents and the second game was a more imposing test, with reigning champions Liverpool the visitors to Elland Road.

Leeds had played well at Villa, fighting back from a goal down, but the popular view among the critics was still that they would do well to avoid relegation. Liverpool represented the acid test for Don Revie's young guns, still without Alan Peacock, sidelined by a knee injury.

Revie stuck with the eleven who defeated Villa, with Don Weston continuing to deputise for Peacock.

Chairman Harry Reynolds rubbed his hands in anticipation of a bumper day at the turnstiles.

Rob Bagchi and Paul Rogerson commented,

> He couldn't help getting carried away, and ... gleefully prepared for the first capacity crowd at Elland Road since the 1920s. The club had reverted to their premium pricing policy, and this time the lack of protest seemed to indicate that the increases were thought justified.
>
> Reynolds' misplaced optimism had potentially disastrous consequences for the fans that did bother to turn up. His expectation of at least a 50,000 attendance led to the paddock stands being crammed full while vast swathes of terracing behind the goals were left vacant for all the non-existent latecomers. One fan complained that the crush was so intense he feared for his life; conditions, others claimed, were 'like the black hole of Calcutta'. Luckily for a penitent Reynolds, there were no major casualties.

When play kicked off, Liverpool adopted their normal approach, with reserve Phil Chisnall taking Ian St John's customary deep-lying No. 9 role, leaving Hunt and Wallace to forage up front.

Leeds worked hard to get into the contest with Billy Bremner and Norman Hunter showing strongly, and Bobby Collins creating havoc. According to the *Yorkshire Post*'s Eric Stanger, it was the respective pace of the two teams that set them apart – Liverpool 'played rather too studiedly, often too short and too square', while 'Leeds used the longer ball for the most part and by constantly switching the direction of attack often pulled a slow-moving Liverpool defence out of position.'

Liverpool showed the calm assurance of champions, confident that they would weather the storm, but were stretched, having a lucky escape before United took the lead in the sixteenth minute: full-back Gerry Byrne attempted a back-pass under pressure from Don Weston, but goalkeeper Tommy Lawrence could do nothing as the ball struck a post. The Scottish custodian was similarly helpless when Johanneson's shot from the edge of the 18-yard box hit Ron Yeats on the shoulder and kicked up and under the bar to register a fortunate opener.

United hopes were dimmed eight minutes later when they were undone by a quick Liverpool combination. Sprake caught a downward header from Hunt after the England man connected with a short centre from Callaghan, but the keeper collided with Reaney as he fell and spilled the ball into the net.

Liverpool were being outfought and outplayed; they were slow to react to an attack five minutes before the break and Weston nodded home from Storrie's centre to give Leeds a 2-1 interval lead.

The excitable Leeds crowd was in ecstasy as the ten minutes after the break saw their heroes assume an emphatic 4-1 lead.

Both goals came from combination work by Giles and Bremner, described by the *Yorkshire Post*'s Eric Stanger as 'little less than a human dynamo'. First the Irishman pulled the ball back for Bremner to beat Lawrence with a powerful drive and then the Scot rolled a free-kick to Giles to hammer home from 30 yards.

There was some late anxiety with the Reds pulling a goal back after seventy minutes. Milne forced home the rebound after Sprake pushed his initial penalty kick onto a post following Bremner's foul on Hunt, but it was Liverpool who became the more ragged outfit in the closing stages.

There were near misses and close calls, but United saw out the threat to secure a historic 4-2 triumph.

Bremner had been at the heart of everything and relished performing on the big stage. He recalled:

We had to perform in front of our own supporters and give them the confidence that we were as good as anyone else in the First Division. Our win at Villa Park had definitely convinced us that we could get results, but we wanted more than that. Our sights were firmly set a lot higher than just survival. Liverpool were a magnificent side. Bill Shankly had transformed them into a very special outfit and we knew they were coming to Elland Road intent on securing maximum points. We had also been made aware that the point of Shankly's psychology was to convince his players that they were playing against a bunch of nobodies, half of whom were limping. He was a canny guy and a brilliant manager and everyone respected him tremendously, but we also rated our own manager and we knew that he would have us prepared to take on and beat anybody.

Liverpool came to Elland Road as reigning champions. Don Revie told us to go out and prove that we were a match, and more, for them. His words inspired us and put us in exactly the right frame of mind for the task ahead. It was quite a task, of course, but we settled quickly ahead and played the way we had performed in the second half against Villa. Liverpool were excellent – as good as we had expected – but we were not going to pay them too much respect and I think they were uneasy long before we were because the unflappable Ron Yeats scored our first goal for us. I pulled his leg about that later. As a fellow Scot, I got away with it.

I don't believe we openly classed the Liverpool game as any different from any other League clash, although it's nice to beat the reigning champions. The supporters were relishing the chance to see us match them. Privately, I think the boss and the rest of us saw it as a benchmark of how we would cope with life in the First Division. It was a great game to play in, a real battle from start to finish, and something else to win 4-2. We left the field that night absolutely drained but emotionally high. The belief and confidence we gained from that one result set us up for the rest of the season.

These were early days in a momentous campaign, but United were one of five teams with maximum points after the first two rounds of fixtures. As Phil Brown remarked: 'Only time and a few more results to match, of course, will really tell, but last night's match could set even this fickle city alight.' How right he was!

Elland Road
Attendance: 36,005

Leeds United: Sprake, Reaney, Bell, Bremner, Charlton, Hunter, Giles, Weston, Storrie, Collins, Johanneson

Liverpool: Lawrence, Byrne, Moran, Milne, Yeats, Stevenson, Callaghan, Hunt, Chisnall, Wallace, Thompson

Everton 0-1 Leeds United
First Division
7 November 1964

There is no way of pinning down exactly when the infamous myth of 'Dirty Leeds' began: it could have been in the spring of 1962 when Bobby Collins was signed; it might have been over Christmas 1963, when players on both sides indulged in onfield thuggery of the worst kind as United clashed twice with promotion rivals Sunderland; or perhaps the month before, when a game with Preston was so aggressive that the referee halted the game after an hour to give the players a chance to calm down.

Whatever the truth, one fixture in November 1964 ranks prominently in the establishment of the legend – United's clash with Everton has gone down as one of English football's most notorious confrontations. It took both sides to generate the heat but the game cemented the Whites' association with controversy and rancour.

Don Revie always strenuously denied that he set out with the intention of his men kicking their way to success, laying the blame instead at the door of opponents, referees, commentators ... anybody outside the confines of Elland Road. However, there are simply too many examples of the Yorkshiremen being involved in appalling scenes for all his protestations of innocence to stand up to objective scrutiny.

The shameless attitude of United's players brought out the worst in others. As often as not, uptight opponents would forget to play football in their eagerness to fight fire with fire and that usually spelled their downfall: United had gained the upper hand, earned the right to dictate terms and usually finished off their opponents with equal measures of skill and brutality. It mattered not which weapon was required – Revie's men were as adept with bludgeon as rapier.

The mood at the time was uncompromising. Revie's paranoid siege mentality came spilling over when he heard the news that the Football Association had named United 'the dirtiest side in the country'. The FA were determined to address the game's worsening discipline and their official journal, the *FA News*, carried an article examining the disciplinary records of its membership. Leeds were highlighted as the Football League club with the worst record for players cautioned, censured, fined or suspended.

United reacted angrily, pointing out that it was not the first team, but their junior sides, that were responsible for the bulk of the numbers.

Revie feared an over-reaction from opponents and certainly that was how it worked out at Goodison Park.

Leeds were the form team with four straight victories. Everton, without a win in a month, remained a class act, eager to put United in their place.

Goodison Park has never been exactly placid; Jack Charlton rated the Everton crowd as 'the worst before which I have ever played ... there always seems to be a threatening attitude, a vicious undertone to their remarks.'

United had tangled with Everton in the FA Cup nine months earlier, and had taken them to a replay before going out in a ferocious clash. For many of his former teammates, memories of Bobby Collins' readiness to take liberties were still fresh, and they awaited United with trepidation.

The game was only seconds old when Everton centre forward Fred Pickering was fouled by Billy Bremner. Seconds later Jack Charlton suffered a similar fate at the hands of an opponent. The battle lines were drawn – this was going to be a tasty affair.

In the fourth minute Johnny Giles and Everton left-back Sandy Brown clashed; when Brown got up and punched Giles, he was immediately dismissed, complaining bitterly of stud marks in his chest.

Somewhere amid the fearsome conflagration, there was a little football being played and after fifteen minutes Leeds took the lead. From a free-kick out on the right, Collins swung the ball high into the heart of the Everton area. Willie Bell came running in at speed to meet the ball perfectly, his header flashing into the net with the defence helpless.

The home crowd had been incensed by Brown's dismissal and now they became uncontrollable. Any Leeds player coming within throwing distance ran the risk of being struck by missiles; for Gary Sprake there was no hiding place as his goal was pelted mercilessly.

Things came to a head after thirty-six minutes. Bell and Everton's Derek Temple were following the flight of the ball and seemingly unaware of each other. They collided at full speed, laying each other out. That was the signal for the crowd to go berserk. While Bell and Temple received attention, missiles rained down; Les Cocker and referee Ken Stokes were struck by flying coins.

Desperate to quell a potential riot, Stokes took drastic action, ordering the players to the dressing rooms to give them and the crowd time to cool off.

It was some minutes before Bell came around sufficiently for Cocker and his teammates to carry him off, while Temple required a stretcher.

For a time, nobody knew whether the game had been suspended or abandoned. Shortly, the loudspeakers announced that play would restart in five minutes, although Stokes warned that the match would be called off if more missiles were thrown.

The game resumed after a ten-minute gap 'on a pitch festooned with the cushions and rubbish thrown by the crowd ... amid a storm of jeers and catcalls'. Both Bell and Temple were back in action, seemingly none the worse for wear. The break did little to assuage the prickliness.

After the resumption, some of the tackling, particularly by Norman Hunter and Roy Vernon, was brutal in the extreme and the match continued to seethe with an undercurrent of barely concealed aggression. Hunter was booked, and the referee lectured Bremner, Collins, Vernon and Stevens for dangerous play. Several players were fortunate to avoid joining Brown in the dressing room.

Collins became dominant, relishing the kind of hostile environment in which he thrived. He ensured that United made the most of their man advantage, exhorting his troops to stretch the game and force Everton to work hard for any possession.

Jack Charlton proved what a resolute and accomplished stopper he had become and received steadfast support from Bremner, Hunter, Bell and Reaney. United manfully resisted the Merseysiders' closing assault as they went all-out for an equaliser. Everton were kept at arm's length as United squeezed out a 1-0 result. The Yorkshiremen had to contend not only with some breakneck football from the home side in the closing minutes, but also with fierce antagonism from the 40,000 Scousers in the crowd.

Billy Bremner was confronted by a home fan as he left the field; he had been at the heart of several nasty moments, though he had been far from an instigator, a point emphasised by Phil Brown in the *Yorkshire Evening Post*: 'Bremner, hunted by Roy Vernon from the start, had a great game in both defence and attack, controlling his temper against heavy fouls both given and overlooked.'

Bremner: 'The tackles were going in as if it was a matter of life and death and tempers, already frayed at the start, were completely lost as the game wore on. There were professional footballers out there who had completely forgotten what they were there for. The ball was actually getting in the way of revenge missions.'

The frightening scenes provoked some predictably hysterical press coverage and raised the hackles of football's establishment. Football League president Joe Richards hinted at firm action to follow, convinced that the growing preoccupation with money was at the root of football's ills.

In the end, the only punishment meted out by the FA was against Everton. Sandy Brown was suspended for two weeks and Everton was fined £250 for the behaviour of their supporters.

The game established the reputation of Revie's United for years to come – they were a bunch of thuggish yobs who would stop at nothing to win a football match. Leeds came out of the game vilified and unloved.

Goodison Park
Attendance: 43,605

Everton: Rankin, Rees, Brown, Gabriel, Labone, Stevens, Temple, Young, Pickering, Vernon, Morrissey

Leeds United: Sprake, Reaney, Bell, Bremner, Charlton, Hunter, Giles, Storrie, Belfitt, Collins, Johanneson

Manchester United 0-0 Leeds United
FA Cup Semi-Final
27 March 1965

As the two Uniteds of Manchester and Leeds came together in the semi-final of the FA Cup in March 1965, their records in the famous old competition could scarcely have been more contrasting.

Leeds had only once before gone as far as the last eight, when John Charles was centre half in a side that came close to beating mighty Arsenal in 1950. The Yorkshire club's normal fate was an early exit and the ten seasons between 1953 and 1962 had yielded not a single victory, an astonishingly tepid record by any standards.

By contrast, the Red Devils had won the Cup on three occasions and had finished runners up twice during the fifties. Add in five League championship successes and one can appreciate exactly how much richer their history was than that of their humble opponents. The Peacocks could point to only two Second Division championships.

However, as the two sides prepared for the Cup showdown, they were separated by just a single point in the chase for the First Division title.

The Yorkshiremen's rise under Don Revie had been startling, and they could point to a win earlier in the season at Old Trafford. That December victory had come during a lengthy unbeaten run, now extended to twenty games after a 4-1 victory against Everton.

The two sides did not care for each other at all. The Yorkshire United were the classic outsiders, kicking at the doors of the feast. Matt Busby's classy eleven considered their opponents uncouth and not fit to be on the same pitch as them.

George Best's recollection was typical of the Manchester perspective: 'That Leeds team are now remembered as the most cynical football team of all time. Although they did deserve that reputation, I hated playing against them, I really did, it must be remembered that they also had a hell of a lot of skill, too, but they were still a bloody nightmare.'

For Best, Paul Reaney came to be a feared spectre at the feast over the years; he was usually detailed to man mark the gifted Irishman, and had done so successfully during the match between the two teams in December. But Best had enjoyed even closer attention from another player, as recounted by Rob Bagchi and Paul Rogerson in *The Unforgiven*:

George Best gives a good example from that Old Trafford encounter of their adventurous aggression: 'As the two teams walked down the tunnel ... I felt a terrific pain in my right calf as someone kicked me with brute force. I turned. It was Bobby Collins. "And that's just for starters, Bestie," he said.' Reprehensible, obviously, and entirely contrary to the spirit of the game, but one can't help being amused by the sheer audacity of the man – and the naked malevolence of the act.

Collins knew that fear worked. If a player is intimidated, the likelihood is that he will give his opponent more time – a footballer's most precious commodity. Collins took it further than most would dare, far too far for some tastes, but it was highly effective. Over the next five years, as Manchester United conquered Europe and George Best was at his peak, he tore countless teams to shreds, but for all his sublime ability he never once dominated a game against Leeds United. It wasn't because Best was physically frightened by Leeds, simply that Leeds were prepared to use every weapon at their disposal to stop him playing, whether physical, psychological, tactical or, like the tunnel assault, borderline criminal.

But it wasn't a cowardly approach. Nobby Stiles, Best's protector-in-chief, took his teammate's revenge. 'Every time you come down our right-hand side and kick George, you filthy b*****d,' he shouted at Collins, slamming him into the perimeter wall in a forceful tackle, 'I'm going to friggin' well hit you like that, only harder.' Collins got up to score the only goal of the game. He had started it, taken the retribution as fair punishment, continued to hound Best despite Stiles' injunctions and still led his team to maximum points. That was the hyperactive impudence that came to characterise Revie's Leeds.

Both teams were at full strength for a match played in front of a capacity 65,000 crowd at Hillsborough, and from the first seconds it was clear that this was to be war, as reported in *The Times*:

> This was a rough and tumble: tough, with the rumble of trouble from the start when Bremner sawed down R. Charlton in full flight. The English player usually is the gentlest of creatures. But now he retaliated immediately in anger, wagged his finger in admonition and from that first act the battle quickly slipped into a black mood that only matched the dark stage itself, a heavy churned up pitch made sticky by heavy overnight rain.
>
> Manchester, having heard of the dog's bad name, clearly were themselves determined not to be bitten. But, in wishing to be master, some of them took matters too far and in the end it was Leeds, paradoxically, who were more sinned against than sinning as a final ratio of three infringements against the one in their favour showed.

Bremner's early assaults on Law and Charlton were provocative catalysts for a fraught atmosphere, but it was the Leeds man who suffered most during the opening twenty minutes. He was felled on several occasions, once rising with a bloodied nose, and shortly afterwards nearly scoring an own goal as he volleyed Connelly's centre from two yards out. He was constantly in the heat of battle and at the heart of most of the game's flashpoints, as was his custom, but he held his cool well in the face of some fearsome tactics and rather enjoyed the no quarters asked contest.

Bremner said,

> I was being kicked all over the place by Paddy Crerand and little Nobby Stiles ... I took what I could until it was time to put a stop to it. It was a bit of a tame challenge that caused me to have a go in return. Paddy had been winding me up all the game, kicking at my calves and grabbing my shirt, holding tight onto me so I couldn't move.
>
> I decided to have a dig back at him, it was a simple elbow to his ribs, not hard but just a reminder that he shouldn't mess with me. Then it all kicked off, name calling, slapping,

shirt pulling, but there was not one punch thrown, we had far too much respect for each other to punch. Everything else was okay, but no punching.

It was soon apparent that this was not to be a flowing game as the teams dug in for trench warfare. Stiles played sweeper for Manchester, while Reaney, Bremner and Hunter were preoccupied with preventing Best, Law and Charlton from making any positive contribution. There was neither time nor space for anybody to get control of the game or display any skill. When a player attempted to do so, they were left in no doubt that savage retribution would be exacted for their impudence.

In an ugly first half Leeds restricted themselves to launching free-kicks high into the Manchester goal area for Peacock, Charlton and Bell to contest. Unfortunately, goalkeeper Pat Dunne had an exemplary game and dealt confidently with everything coming his way.

When the Peacocks tried a more cultured approach, feeding Giles and Johanneson on the flanks, both men were brutally dealt with, Stiles being the main enforcer.

Things degenerated in the second half, with Stiles and Crerand leaving Johanneson a limping passenger, while Bremner did the same to Best. With Peacock checked by Foulkes, and Law and Bobby Charlton more concerned with demonstrating their tackling than attacking flair, the game slumped into a bitter dogfight.

Stiles and Law were booked for bad fouls on Johanneson and Bell, and the only surprise was that more players were not cautioned or even dismissed.

There was one clash after an hour that transcended everything that had gone before and referee Dick Windle bottled it, declining to take the action that was required to get the game under control. Denis Law went chasing after Jack Charlton, seemingly intent on making a point. He caught up with the centre half and blocked him forcefully. Charlton lost his temper and fists started flying. The flare up was the signal for the pent-up anger of all the warriors to be vented, and players from both sides piled in. Crerand and Bremner clashed violently and Stiles and Hunter had to be physically separated.

It was several minutes before calm was restored, with Law's shredded shirt left hanging loosely from his shoulder for the rest of the contest. Windle took no action, choosing only to tick Law off and award a free-kick to Leeds. His tolerance was inexplicable.

The match rumbled to a goalless conclusion, with the balance of fouls twenty-four by Manchester to ten by Leeds. There was an air of apprehension about what would ensue in the replay, with several scores to be settled.

Hillsborough
Attendance: 65,000

Manchester United: P. Dunne, Brennan, A. Dunne, Crerand, Foulkes, Stiles, Connelly, R. Charlton, Herd, Law, Best

Leeds United: Sprake, Reaney, Bell, Bremner, J. Charlton, Hunter, Giles, Storrie, Peacock, Collins, Johanneson

Manchester United 0-1 Leeds United
FA Cup Semi-Final Replay
31 March 1965

After the rancorous first clash against Manchester United, Eric Stanger reported in the *Yorkshire Post*: 'Perhaps it is as well there is a replay at Nottingham on Wednesday. At least it will give both sides opportunity to show that they can play good football and redeem themselves for a shabby, bitter FA Cup semi-final at Hillsborough on Saturday … Altogether too many players on both sides behaved like a pack of dogs snapping and snarling at each other over a bone.'

Despite fitness doubts on both sides following the bruising encounter, the only change was Terry Cooper replacing the injured Albert Johanneson on the Leeds left wing. Cooper had been unlucky to miss the first match through injury having featured regularly over recent weeks as either left-back or left winger, and the bloody-minded assaults on Johanneson at the weekend made Cooper's recall a formality.

Referee Dick Windle, heavily criticised for losing control of the first game, was officiating again and determined to take a firmer approach; his changed approach reaped rewards. There were again far too many fouls, twenty against the Mancunians and five against the Whites, but most were for petty offences.

Matters were helped by improved playing conditions. At Hillsborough, the players had to contend with a bog of a pitch, sticky and holding and mitigating against expansive play. Nottingham's City Ground offered a fast, dry surface.

Once again, Leeds were content to rely on their defensive excellence to see them through, with Bobby Collins dominant. The *Yorkshire Evening Post*'s Phil Brown noted that Collins 'was again invaluable, pulling United out of trouble at one end of the field, and touching off their attacking at the other'. Billy Bremner stood ably at the side of the older man, offering dynamic assistance.

Manchester appeared determined to make up for missing out first time around, but after their opening burst, Leeds came into the picture. With Johnny Giles growing in influence, the Whites went close on several occasions, most of their chances coming from high balls into the Manchester penalty area for Alan Peacock to contest.

Busby's men started the better after the break, but this time their dominance was total and for the first twenty minutes there was only one side in it.

Gradually, the storm abated, and the Yorkshiremen sensed that the Mancunians were beginning to doubt they could pierce the resilient defence.

Don Revie was never one to let an opportunity pass him by. Sensing that Busby's men were fading, he issued his orders to capitalise. He pulled Giles back to a deeper central role, moved Storrie out wide on the right and thrust Bremner forward as an auxiliary attacker. Bell and Reaney were encouraged to push forward on the wings.

The tide had turned. At first, Leeds merely held their own, but as the game moved into its fateful last quarter, they came to dominate matters.

The seconds ticked by with still no goals to show for all the effort, and the lottery of extra time beckoned. As the match moved into its final two minutes, Stiles floored Bremner with a late tackle in the centre circle, seemingly happy to trade a long-range free-kick to prevent a quick break. Giles floated the ball unerringly into the heart of a crowded goal area.

Bremner, mind working overtime, weighed things up more speedily than his opponents. He flashed past three or four defenders and moved in on the steepling place kick. With his back to goal, he twisted artfully under the ball and nudged it with his head past Pat Dunne, through a tiny chink in the defensive wall and into the top corner of the net.

For milliseconds that seemed an eternity there was an eerie silence before an explosion of noise. Without quite understanding how he got there, Bremner found himself out on the touchline, being mobbed by excited teammates, in celebration of what was certain to be the winning goal.

Bremner said,

At first I thought Johnny had taken it too quickly and overhit it. I remember reacting first and seeing the Manchester United defenders stood still. I was thinking 'f*** me, I'm in mid-air leaping like a salmon, and that f***ing ball is going to sail right past me and out of play.' As it dropped, I realised I could get my head to it and said to myself, 'Go on, Bill, head the f***ing thing into the net, you can reach it, you can do it.' The ball seemed to drop down in its trajectory, beside, yet behind, my head. I twisted myself backwards and sideways in mid-air, and managed to divert it into the Manchester United goal!

To this very day I still don't know how I got to that ball, yet as soon as I did, I knew it was going in. Johnny always said he had dropped it right on my head. That's not true. He hit it in my general direction.

The Red Devils tried a last-ditch, all-out assault to regain equality, but Leeds were in no mood to surrender their advantage and repelled the feverish attacks.

When referee Windle blew his whistle to signal the end, the crowd swarmed onto the pitch. Windle was struck by a Reds supporter and fell to the ground, requiring attention from ambulance men and protection from the police as the culprit was apprehended.

The Leeds party was just beginning; oblivious to what was going on around them, they celebrated furiously. As commentator Kenneth Wolstenholme remarked memorably, 'Don Revie's gone mad!'

Billy Bremner had led from the front as Eric Stanger reported in the *Yorkshire Post*: 'Leeds had no stars in the sense that any one man was outstanding, but Bremner, apart from his goal, had one of his greatest games, covering at one time and another almost every inch of the field in stopping raids and starting them.'

City Ground, Nottingham
Attendance: 46,300

Manchester United: P. Dunne, Brennan, A. Dunne, Crerand, Foulkes, Stiles, Connelly, R. Charlton, Herd, Law, Best

Leeds United: Sprake, Reaney, Bell, Bremner, J. Charlton, Hunter, Giles, Storrie, Peacock, Collins, Cooper

Birmingham City 3-3 Leeds United
First Division
26 April 1965

Leeds United had exceeded the hopes of even their most optimistic supporters, coming closer to silverware in twelve short months than their predecessors had managed in the other forty-five years of the club's existence.

As they faced Birmingham in their final League game, they were still chasing the double, but their title challenge had stalled. A run of poor results had allowed long-time favourites Manchester United to regain the advantage.

After an eighteen-match unbeaten run in the League, and a single defeat in twenty-seven, Leeds had surrendered their lead at the top following Manchester's victory at Elland Road on 17 April. When Leeds crashed 3-0 at Sheffield Wednesday two days later, matters seemed cut and dried. Faint Yorkshire hopes were revived, however, by impressive victories over the following five days against the two Sheffield clubs.

It remained a major ask – Leeds' Monday evening fixture at Birmingham was their fifth match in ten days. They were a point clear, but the Mancunians enjoyed a game in hand and a superior goal average.

Leeds had to go all-out for victory and, even then, they would have to rely on Busby's side dropping points, either at home that same evening to Arsenal, or a couple of nights later at Aston Villa. The chances of Villa doing Leeds a favour were remote – they had earlier crashed 7-0 at Old Trafford.

Birmingham had endured a disastrous campaign, winning just seven games and already doomed to finish bottom after Manchester's 4-2 win at St Andrews a week earlier. It looked a straightforward task for Leeds to complete their half of mission impossible.

However, United started tentatively, and fell behind after four minutes – City outside-left Dennis Thwaites scored after being put clear by Terry Hennessey. Two minutes later, Manchester United took the lead against Arsenal through a wonder goal from George Best.

Another minute gone, and Birmingham winger Alex Jackson went off with a suspected dislocated shoulder after a clash with Terry Cooper, roundly booed every time he touched the ball thereafter.

Eric Stanger in the *Yorkshire Post*: 'Leeds, though their football was often fretful with anxiety, should have had the game in their keeping by half-time. Peacock missed two good chances, the first from Giles and the second from Hunter's pass, while Weston hooked wide with the Birmingham defence waiting for the whistle to go for offside. The nearest Leeds got to a goal in that half was when Giles carved out a chance for himself only for Schofield to leave his goal in a desperate dash and parry the outside-right's shot.'

The break did nothing to disrupt Birmingham's momentum and they took a 3-0 lead six minutes after the restart.

They mounted two attacks and converted both. Beard got the first after Geoff Vowden had cleverly flicked on a centre from Hennessey and Vowden made it three when he turned a long through pass from Malcolm Page past Sprake.

Nine minutes later, Denis Law increased Manchester United's lead to two goals just as Arsenal were threatening a rally. Resigned to their fate, Don Revie passed on a message to 'take it steady'.

However, Leeds misunderstood the manager's signals and from somewhere the famous Yorkshire fighting spirit returned to breathe fire into their game.

Billy Bremner: 'The boss told us to take it easy because of the Cup final and we took him at his word. We went 3-0 down. Then I suddenly saw him on the touchline waving his arms about. You don't really hear what people are saying to you from off the pitch, but we got the message that he wanted us to get back into the game. We started to put the foot on the accelerator.'

As had happened several times over recent weeks, Bremner moved up front. After sixty-five minutes, City left-back Green brought the Scot down in the area, and Giles coolly converted the penalty to pull one goal back.

Minutes later, George Eastham did the same at Old Trafford to haul Arsenal back into the other contest.

Those incidents were the catalyst for the high drama that ensued over the last twenty minutes, as Leeds threw themselves into kitchen sink attack.

In the seventy-third minute, an intensive bombardment of the Birmingham goal ended with Reaney hammering the first League goal of his career. With the score now at 3-2, the momentum was all with Leeds as the crowd in Manchester started to chew their nails. There was a hint that this could yet be an incredible evening for Yorkshire.

Jack Charlton thumped home an equaliser two minutes from the end, throwing Birmingham into a panic. With virtually everyone camped in the City area, Norman Hunter smashed the ball against a post in injury time.

There was to be no salvation, and the game ended in a breathless 3-3 draw.

In the closing minutes at Old Trafford, Denis Law tapped in a third to confirm Manchester as 3-1 victors. There was still a remote mathematical possibility that their positions could be reversed (Aston Villa would need to have scored 19 against the Reds in the final match to have given Leeds a superior goal average), but the game was up – Busby's club was crowned League champions for the sixth time in their history.

In that final match, Villa beat Manchester United 2-1, leaving Leeds as runners up by dint of goal average. Their points total of sixty-one was the highest ever achieved by a team failing to win the title, and enough to have won the championship on all but three occasions since the war. If truth be known, the Red Devils would probably have gained the points at Villa if they had needed them, but Leeds had come desperately close to glory.

All the plaudits and congratulations of well-wishers came as little consolation to a desperately disappointed set of players. They had come within a whisker of footballing immortality; if anyone had offered them a chance of runners up spot twelve months previously, the Whites would have bitten their hand off, but now it felt like a hollow achievement.

St Andrews
Attendance: 16,644

Birmingham City: Schofield, Lynn, Green, Hennessey, Foster, Page, Jackson, Martin, Vowden, Beard, Thwaites

Leeds United: Sprake, Reaney, Cooper, Bremner, Charlton, Hunter, Giles, Weston, Peacock, Collins, Johanneson

Liverpool 2-1 Leeds United
FA Cup Final
1 May 1965

As consolation for missing out to Manchester United in the pursuit of the League title, Leeds could still look forward to an FA Cup final appearance against reigning champions Liverpool. It was United's first sniff of Cup glory, and, with the Anfield club never having won the Cup, it was certain there would be a new name on the trophy.

Leeds were narrow favourites but there were far more red favours in the Wembley crowd than white, and Don Revie's young side was unusually uptight as they came out of the tunnel. Bill Shankly turned to his old Merseyside adversary, Bobby Collins, and asked him how he was. Collins answered, 'I feel awful,' capturing the mood of his team.

The tension has never been adequately explained but it was unquestionable – Leeds were there in body but not in spirit. They simply froze.

Fellow Scots Collins and Ron Yeats came forward for the toss, polar opposites in height with fully 12 inches between them. The United captain called correctly, opting to change ends and allow the Reds to kick-off.

Liverpool, battle-hardened from three years in the top flight and twelve months of European competition, were assured from the start, fluid and flexible. They played within themselves, content to maintain possession rather than risk the gamble of a panicky forward pass. Their formation alternated smoothly between 4-4-2 and 4-2-4, founded on the midfield control of Geoff Strong and Willie Stevenson. The forwards were in perpetual shuttle, offering width and the constant option of a short square pass. They retained possession courtesy of easy passing triangles around pedestrian opponents. The speed and ease with which Ian St John and Roger Hunt combined in slick and smooth one-twos left Jack Charlton and Norman Hunter nonplussed.

United were as rigid and static as the stance of Alan Peacock, constantly outthought and outmanoeuvred: their defence, tantalised by Liverpool's patterns and movement, entrenched on the edge of their area; Billy Bremner, Johnny Giles and Collins clustered tightly in midfield, content to move as a unit but with only the long ball as an outlet; Albert Johanneson, strangely out of sorts, and Jim Storrie, rendered immobile and ineffective by early injury, made only fitful contributions, leaving Peacock alone and exposed, dominated by the looming Yeats.

United's midfield trio were caught between two stools, either stranded upfield, leaving Liverpool an acre of room to exploit and their back four dreadfully exposed, or too remote from their forwards to bring them into the game in a meaningful way.

It was frustrating; the stage had been set for Johanneson to deliver the performance that would take the cause of the black footballer in Britain to fresh heights. He could have cemented his reputation as one of the most exciting wingers in the game, but he froze. He was the one Leeds player who could excite crowds, but Liverpool handled him superbly, with Lawler sitting deep and waiting for the South African to commit himself. The normal outcome was the ball bouncing loose and Lawler picking off his man.

Gary Sprake was the one Leeds player to shine, though Bremner ran his heart out in the United cause. Sprake saved countless efforts and kept his team in the contest far longer than they deserved.

The match fell far short of its billing, but that was unsurprising. Few teams were better equipped to drive the colour out of an occasion than Leeds and Liverpool. The two sides had made their mark on the First Division with their system and method football, which the physical rigours of Division Two had demanded. They were spearheading a grim trend in the English game, as declaimed in one quote at the time:

> The leaden football of the first 90 minutes has earned the 1965 Cup final a reputation as the worst final for years. This is the price the public must pay for the success it demands. Gates for years have shown that the fans will not settle for brave losers; they ought not now to complain of the way victories are won. Leeds and Liverpool did not play like this because they were at Wembley. Rather, they were at Wembley precisely because they play like this.
>
> Like it or loathe it, this was the football that got them there. I am astonished to find so many surprised at the style and standard of the play. Almost alone on Saturday, I warned that this method football would come strange to the taste of many. Too late, the English are finding that you cannot have the prize without that play. It is like a man swapping his battered sports car for the efficiency and comfort of a saloon, then complaining he misses the exhilarating rush of wind in his face.

In the opening minutes, Collins stamped into a challenge on Byrne, intent on giving Liverpool reason to fear for their lives. Play was held up for two minutes as Byrne received treatment. He recalled later: 'I went in for a tackle with Bobby Collins. He put his foot over the ball and turned his shoulder into me. I'd never broken a collarbone before, so I wasn't aware of what damage had been done straight away. It didn't cross my mind to leave the field and I played on with my arm dangling motionless by my side.'

Byrne masked his discomfort so completely that no one knew until the end that he had broken a bone. In fact, he gave a wonderful performance, slick and assured, earning himself the time and space to avoid further damage.

Charlton, Bremner and Storrie all required Les Cocker's attention within ten minutes of the start. Storrie's damaged left ankle eventually left him a hobbling passenger on the right wing.

Only once in the first twenty minutes did Leeds threaten, when Bremner won the ball and released Johanneson wide on the left. He made some progress and the overlapping Bell won a corner, but Peacock's header was aimless and wide. The telling pass from Bremner was a rarity from United. Most of their contributions were long and aimless, pumped down the middle for the head of Peacock, and easily snuffed out by Yeats. Had his colleagues learned from Bremner's example, or had Johanneson been more effective with the little possession he enjoyed, Leeds might have fared better, but neither came to pass.

In stark contrast, St John and Hunt, prompted by the canny control of Stevenson, exploited the space in front of United's back four and carved out decent opportunities.

Rain began to fall heavily after twenty-five minutes, making conditions difficult. Liverpool continued to have the better of things but there was not even the hint of a goal in a drab first half.

Liverpool grew more dominant after the break and came close several times, forcing Sprake into action time and again. On occasions the United defence were camped in their own area, Liverpool's slick pass-and-move approach stretching them to the limit.

Bremner pushed forward in the latter stages as Storrie grew more uncomfortable, and brought some much-needed fire, if few opportunities.

Liverpool seemed a little too ready to hold possession as they shifted crablike across the field, but they were always able to forge an opening. Charlton and Hunter blocked many efforts, and Sprake was outstanding.

Hunt headed Callaghan's centre over the bar; Charlton blocked a ten-yard drive from St John; Stevenson fluffed his shot after a free-kick bounced clear; Callaghan fired into the side netting from long range out on the right, before Thompson went even closer after bursting in from the other wing.

Surely Leeds would concede sooner or later? But they didn't, and somehow managed to reach ninety minutes with a clean sheet. They had never come close to a goal themselves, despite all Bremner's urgency, yet they were a durable nut to crack.

It was the first time since 1947 that extra time had been required, and the way things were going there was a suspicion that there might be the first replay since 1912.

United kicked off the extra thirty minutes with Bremner conspicuously leading the attack and Johanneson switching wings, but the break had disturbed United's concentration. Stevenson slipped through several tackles as he danced deftly towards the edge of the Leeds area and slid an incisive through ball to the overlapping Byrne. The full-back's clipped ball from the byline was nodded in by a stooping Hunt to send the Scousers into raptures.

Liverpool should have safely seen out the game, but Leeds contrived to create their best opening after nine minutes of extra time.

Giles brought down a lofted Liverpool clearance on the touchline, playing it to Peacock who fed Hunter. The defender, advancing to the edge of the centre circle, launched the ball into the penalty area for Charlton to nod back. The advancing Bremner met the dropping ball on the volley and fired home.

There were no more goals in the first period, but Liverpool launched several assaults as play resumed. Sprake saved Strong's shot from the edge of the area and then Hunter volleyed clear for a corner when St John got away inside the box. Leeds couldn't hold out and after six minutes of the second period, Liverpool regained the lead.

Thompson gained possession out on the left and fed Smith, who shipped it on to Callaghan on the right. He rounded Bell, skipped to the byline and centred for the plunging St John to net in fine style.

Leeds broke back and for once Johanneson made a decent surge only for Bremner to be flagged for offside, signalling the end of United's effort.

Just afterwards Charlton lost possession to Thompson as he was carrying forward, and the winger broke away at speed. He advanced to the edge of the area and jinked left to create some space, before letting fly. His shot brought the best out of Sprake.

The tired limbs could offer no more resistance. Liverpool saw out the remaining minutes comfortably to earn their first Cup triumph, sending Leeds back to Yorkshire with nothing to show for a wonderful season.

Billy Bremner: 'Having drawn level, we should have pulled everyone back into defence and concentrated on getting a draw. We would then have been able to polish up our game before the replay – I am sure that we couldn't possibly have played so badly a second time. But that equaliser prompted us to go for victory, and in doing so, I feel we handed victory to Liverpool on a plate.'

Don Revie promised his players they would be back, telling Bremner: 'Don't let it worry you, Billy. We will be back and next time you'll be skipper and we'll win.' But for now his players were alone with only their disappointment for company.

Wembley Stadium
Attendance: 100,000

Liverpool: Lawrence, Lawler, Byrne, Strong, Yeats, Stevenson, Callaghan, Hunt, St John, Smith, Thompson

Leeds United: Sprake, Reaney, Bell, Bremner, Charlton, Hunter, Giles, Storrie, Peacock, Collins, Johanneson

Scotland 0-0 Spain
Friendly
8 May 1965

It was a proud day for Billy Bremner when he was given his international debut, selected for a friendly at Hampden Park against Spain a week after the Cup final.

Twenty-two-year-old Bremner had already played three times for Scotland Under-23s, his debut coming against England at St James' Park, Newcastle, on 5 February 1964, of which he said,

> My first Scotland honour since I was a boy was a big moment in my career. It felt good to be wearing a Scotland shirt and I hoped that it would be a stepping stone to a full cap. It was a big ambition of mine to play for my country at senior level, even if it was only for one game. The Under-23 international game at Newcastle went against us. Fred Pickering scored a hat-trick for England and they won 3-2. We were disappointed because we really thought we had done enough at least to get a draw.
>
> My next game for the side was at the end of that season. The excitement of winning the Second Division with Leeds was still fresh in my mind when I was asked to put on the Scotland shirt again to face France ... We came away with a creditable 2-0 victory. I don't think anyone expected us to pull off such a result. At best we were expected to grab a draw – but we had done much better than that.

Bremner's full debut saw him lining up alongside Bobby Collins, making his second appearance for the Scots since a six-year exile. The two men shared a passionate will to win and the presence of his club mate soothed any anxiety that Bremner's step up into the full international side might have caused.

Scotland were in the midst of a World Cup qualifying campaign that saw them pitted against Italy, Poland and Finland and they were looking good after a 3-1 victory against the Finns.

Bremner was one of three changes to the team that had drawn 2-2 with England on 10 April, called up with fellow debutant John Hughes of Celtic and Tottenham's Alan Gilzean. He was bursting with pride as he walked out in front of a 60,000-strong Hampden crowd alongside ten compatriots split equally between Anglo Scots and those who continued to ply their trade north of the border.

While the game was one of the most memorable of his career for Bremner, there was to be no special occasion – the game was ill-tempered, notable chiefly for descending into farce when one of the Spaniards was sent off only to see out the ninety minutes because of a refereeing oversight. The offender punched Denis Law before throwing himself to the ground feigning injury.

English referee Kevin Howley was not fooled by his antics and ordered the player off. However, he continued to roll around on the turf in apparent agony as chaos reigned all around him with players from both sides squaring up to each other. Things got so heated that the referee completely forgot the dismissal and allowed the Spaniard to remain on the pitch when order was finally restored.

Spain did, in fact, end the match a man short anyway after Severino Reija was dismissed in the eighty-sixth minute.

The contest ended in a bitty goalless draw, with little coherent football played, though Bremner understandably recalled it as a good game. He thoroughly enjoyed his big day, saying, 'I was a bit disappointed when we didn't win, especially since I was not picked for the next few games – and I took that personally.'

Manager Ian McColl was sacked a few days later after five years in the role, replaced on an interim basis by Celtic boss Jock Stein. It would be five months and four games before an impatient Bremner was given a second cap, though Stein assured him he figured in his long-term plans.

Hampden Park
Attendance: 60,146

Scotland: Brown, Hamilton, McCreadie, Bremner, McNeill, Greig, Henderson, Collins, Law, Gilzean, Hughes

Spain: Iribar, Rivilla, Olivella, Reija, Zoco, Glaria, Ufarte, Aragones, Martinez, Aguirre, Lapetra

14

Torino 0-0 Leeds United
Inter-Cities Fairs Cup: First Round, Second Leg
6 October 1965

In November 1963, United chairman Harry Reynolds announced, 'We not only want to be one of the best clubs in England, but in Europe. We want to be in that Super League if it comes. We do not just wish to get into the First Division but to win it and get into the European Cup.'

At the time, Reynolds' words sounded fanciful but by the autumn of 1965, United were indeed contemplating their European debut, against Torino in the Inter-Cities Fairs Cup.

The Italians were rebuilding after a disastrous air crash in 1949 when their plane hit the church of Superga in the hills over Turin. It was the biggest tragedy in Italian sports history, claiming the lives of a team that had won four successive Series A titles. They struggled to recover and succumbed to relegation in 1959 after a decade of mid-table finishes, but were coming back to prominence under the management of the redoubtable Nereo Rocco. They were hot favourites to beat Leeds.

The first leg at Elland Road on 29 September saw United take to European competition like ducks to water.

Don Revie sent his forwards out in mixed-up shirt numbers to upset Torino's man-marking plans, but the ruse was quickly rumbled by the Italians, who resisted United's opening lunges thanks mainly to goalkeeper Lido Vieri and centre half George Puja.

However, they could not hold out for long. Billy Bremner ('the best player on the field' according to Phil Brown of the *Yorkshire Evening Post*) opened the scoring after twenty-five minutes with a speculative curling shot from the left wing. The Whites had other first half opportunities, but it was the forty-eighth minute before Alan Peacock's header crowned a decent passing move and doubled the advantage. Later Peacock had a goal disallowed, with the referee ruling the ball had not entered the goal, 'though the centre forward was afterwards to claim the ball was a good 18 inches over the line.'

Opting to go for a killer third score rather than sitting on a 2-0 lead, United left themselves exposed and Torino centre forward Orlando pulled a goal back twelve minutes from time.

The away goals rule had yet to be introduced so it would take a victory by two clear goals in Turin to put the Italians through, but most independent experts believed Torino's greater experience would be decisive.

Leeds fielded the same eleven in the second leg while the Italians rang the changes. The return of Gigi Meroni was particularly crucial. The twenty-two-year-old was a

Continental equivalent of George Best. Torino's record buy, he was a prodigious talent, 'a first-rate dribbler and expert at nutmegging his opponents.'

Meroni and George Ferrini were prominent as Torino took the game to United in the early stages, but Leeds manufactured the first chance.

Jack Charlton: 'We could have been a goal up after only thirty seconds, but Peter Lorimer's shot was clutched safely by goalkeeper Vieri; then Vieri clawed a header from me as the ball was sneaking under the bar; and Norman Hunter, put through after a great Lorimer run, missed his kick in front of an open goal.'

The openings were scarce thereafter with Peacock left to plough a lone furrow up front with his fellow forwards supplementing a packed midfield.

In the last five minutes of the half, United had a decent spell, prompted by skipper Bobby Collins. He collected smartly from Peacock and sent in a shot that skimmed a post, before dispossessing Ferrini with a wonderful tackle and swiftly turning defence into attack.

Leeds took their break in good heart, although any degree of complacency was dissipated five minutes after the resumption.

Collins had been United's fulcrum since his arrival in 1962, and in Turin he was again the heartbeat of a defiant display. Unfortunately, he would not see out the hour.

Norman Hunter: 'I can still remember the tackle that put him out of the game ... Bobby and I were both well up the field when I saw a big defender coming towards him. Bobby was extremely quick over 5 to 10 yards and he knocked the ball forward and accelerated after it but the big guy didn't pull up. He kept on running and his knee went right into Bobby's thigh. When I got to Bobby, his leg was waving around at the top because the bone was snapped high up the leg. It was horrendous.'

Billy Bremner said,

I was so upset that I found myself weeping and, had the chance come my way, I would have 'done' the player who had so crippled my teammate.

The foul was quite the worst that I had ever seen and when I realised what had happened, I must admit that I lost my head completely and snarled at the player who had done it, 'I'll kill you for this.' Believe me, I really meant it at the time, too. That player probably didn't understand what I had said, but he certainly got the message and stayed well away from me for the rest of the match. Perhaps it was as well – for me as much as for him!

I have never since that day gone onto the field with such feelings as I had then. That day, blinding anger and passion got the better of me and obscured my better judgement. If I had tangled with that Italian player in a fight for possession of the ball, I could not have been responsible for my actions. The foul had been so unnecessary and was so obviously vindictive – Bobby had been 10 yards from the ball when he had been, quite literally, jumped on.

United were left to withstand forty minutes of all-out pressure with ten men. Substitutes had been introduced for Football League games at the start of the season, but were still some way off for European competition.

But the Italians could find no chinks in the United armour. Gary Sprake made a couple of decent saves, but for the most part his defence kept Torino at arm's length.

The Italians' football grew increasingly frenetic as the end approached, and United came close to snatching a remarkable victory at the death when Bremner burst clear and beat the defence only to watch his shot scrape the post.

The game finished without a goal, leaving United in the second round by virtue of the 2-1 aggregate score.

It was a memorable evening, and the triumph in adversity proved a turning point in United's history. Their football, for so long reviled in England, seemed perfectly designed for the European game.

Shorn of his pocket general, Don Revie gave Johnny Giles his head as playmaker, thereby creating a midfield partnership with Billy Bremner that would inspire United's success over the decade that followed.

Bremner quickly appreciated Giles' value, recalling later,

We clicked almost immediately. Somehow we knew instantly what the other would do and we were able to work together without even talking about it.

I have never known a quieter or more modest player than Johnny Giles. He always did his best to walk away from trouble even though he could look after himself more than adequately if he had to. He just didn't want to lower himself to the level of players who were capable of little more than kicking and punching. It has often been said that Johnny Giles was the most accurate passer of the ball in the game and I would not doubt that.

Collins' injury was not quite the end of the road for him, and he was back for the season's climax, a draw with Manchester United that secured runners up spot.

The return was a short one, however, with Collins signing for Bury in February 1967. His association with Leeds had been a match made in heaven, although many of Collins' opponents might have muttered that it was forged somewhere less pleasant!

Stadio Comunale, Turin
Attendance: 26,000

Torino: Vieri, Poletti, Fossati, Puja, Teneggi, Ferretti, Meroni, Ferrini, Orlando, Pestrin, Simoni

Leeds United: Sprake, Reaney, Madeley, Bremner, Charlton, Hunter, Giles, Lorimer, Peacock, Collins, Cooper

15

Leeds United 1-1 Valencia
Inter-Cities Fairs Cup: Third Round, First Leg
2 February 1966

One of the greatest storms in European football burst about the heads of Leeds United ... I was in the centre of the row – three players, including myself, were ordered off; both teams were also summoned from the field for a spell to allow heated tempers to cool; and when it was all over, Dutch referee Leo Horn claimed: 'Money was the cause of the trouble. You could almost smell it on the pitch.' Such was the chaos and such was the anger that, at the time, our manager, Don Revie, said: 'If this is European football I think we are better out of it'.

Jack Charlton

Leeds were not in the best of states as they approached the game. They had overcome League leaders Liverpool at Anfield over Christmas, but lost 1-0 at Elland Road to the Reds a day later. Although they had three games in hand due to postponements caused by a harsh winter, their 2-0 defeat at Sunderland on 29 January left them in fourth spot, eight points behind the Merseysiders.

Worse still, they didn't have a recognised centre forward following Alan Peacock's knee injury in the first half at Sunderland.

An obvious move would have been to switch Jim Storrie into his old No. 9 role, but he had been playing well on the wide right and was only just recovered from injury himself. In his desperation, Revie considered picking either Billy Bremner or Willie Bell up front, but instead opted for Rod Belfitt in a side that had otherwise become recognised as his first choice. Jack Charlton, acting as captain in the absence of Bobby Collins, missed the defeat at Sunderland with a neck ricked in training, but returned for the game.

Leeds dominated the first half, but struggled to find their normal high-tempo rhythm. Valencia were a knowing force, disrupting United with their possession football, close marking, spoiling tactics and heavy tackling.

Leeds struggled to make headway, with Belfitt out of his depth. They had most of the possession but failed to carve out a clear-cut opening: Giles' free-kick went narrowly wide; then he hurried a shot with the Spanish defence for once looking uncertain; and Nito blocked Lorimer's shot at short range, but that was about it.

Valencia were less wasteful and took the lead after sixteen minutes following a defensive misunderstanding. Leeds were caught short following an attack, and Hunter and Reaney each left things to the other when a speculative long ball dropped into their half.

There was no such hesitation from Munoz and he was on it in a flash, rounding Sprake before slipping the ball home.

Valencia pulled everyone back, allowing United's frenetic assaults to crash against a wall of red shirts.

Refereeing the game was Leo Horn, a renowned Dutch official, who had handled more than 100 internationals, including Hungary's 6-3 defeat of England in 1953. Horn seemed reluctant to impose his authority, offering Valencia enormous latitude, which they shamelessly exploited.

Phil Brown commented in the *Yorkshire Evening Post*:

> Mr Horn should have sensed the lava flow in this game in the first minute when Hunter swept Lage off his feet and Lage looked daggers at Hunter. Mr Horn gave verbal rebuke, appealed to the captains, Charlton and Roberto, but he should have laid down an ultimatum by quarter time, and started booking.
>
> That does not excuse the players for a moment for playing the game in the wrong spirit. Billy Bremner, hunted and fouled with sickening consistency, kept his head magnificently against an evil barrage of tackles, and played his football to the end. He deserves very great praise indeed.

After such a fierce first half, the game restarted peacefully after the break and O'Grady's deep centre nearly caught Nito out before it drifted wide. Things soon heated up, though, as full-back Vidagany flattened Bremner when he tried to make space on the right. The referee beckoned the Valencia captain for another warning, but took no further action.

Bremner's patience in face of such provocation was exemplary; he had not always been able to turn the other cheek like this, but he knew he could not rise to the bait for fear of fatally undermining United's cause.

The Times reported:

> Leeds had been pounding away at Valencia's mobile wall of defenders from the outset of the second half; they desperately needed a steadying influence to harness and channel their drive but what they lacked in imaginative ideas, they substituted with spirit and the Spaniards were seemingly content to contain them. The manner in which they sometimes did so certainly incurred the displeasure of the Leeds fans.
>
> All the shafts, at this stage, were aimed at Leeds: O'Grady's centre eluded Nito and passed wide; Lorimer flung himself at Bremner's centre for the goalkeeper to save; and Storrie's header was, in turn, cleared off the line.
>
> Yet still Leeds hardly suggested they knew how to open up the Valencia defence which, at times, funnelled as many as nine red shirts into the goal area. One had almost begun to despair that the curtain could be pierced when Leeds equalised, Lorimer driving home a cross from Giles. It was certainly reward for the pressure they had brought to bear.

Jack Charlton said:

> Fifteen minutes to go, and I raced upfield to add my weight to one of our attacks. As I challenged an opponent in the Valencia penalty area, I was kicked. This angered

me, of course – but before I knew where I was I found myself having to take much more … for one of my opponents slung a punch which would have done credit to Cassius Clay.

Right there and then my anger boiled over … I chased around that penalty area, intent upon only one thing – getting my own back. I had completely lost control of myself, after these diabolical fouls upon me, and neither the Spaniards nor the restraining hands of my teammates could prevent my pursuit for vengeance. Suddenly players seemed to be pushing and jostling each other everywhere. Police appeared on the field to stop this game of football from degenerating into a running battle. And Leo Horn walked off with his linesmen, signalling to club officials of both teams to get their players off, too.

I was still breathing fire when I reached the dressing room – then I got the word that I need not go back. For a moment I thought the referee had called off the match … then it sank home that it was only Jackie Charlton's presence which was not required any longer. For eleven minutes the teams remained off the field, to allow tempers on both sides to cool down.

The conflict did not end there. Seven minutes from time Valencia, inside forward Sanchez-Lage felled Jim Storrie and was promptly dismissed. That finally calmed the atmosphere.

In the last quarter of an hour, either side might have gained a precious lead, with Sprake having to stretch to tip Guillot's header over the bar and Bremner missing narrowly with a header at the death. In the end, though, the 1-1 draw was just about right. Despite all the furore, United and Valencia had proven themselves well-matched and worthy opponents. They came with wildly different backgrounds and approaches to the game, but it was the devil's own job to separate the two.

The papers inevitably focused on the less savoury side of the contest and there were calls for United to be thrown out of the competition and Charlton to face a lengthy ban.

The Fairs Cup Committee decided to delay their response, meeting the day after the decisive second leg. They made sure it was public knowledge that they would have observers present for the return in Valencia and that behaviour there would colour their final judgement. They had already banned Roma for three years after crowd trouble when they hosted Chelsea earlier in the competition, so were known to be ready to impose the strictest of sanctions.

Leo Horn faced intense criticism for his part in affairs. He had been hopeful of being selected to referee the forthcoming World Cup final, but now kissed goodbye to that opportunity. He was replaced for the second leg, a fortnight later, by Othmar Huber of Switzerland.

From the very start Huber punished the slightest indiscretion and his fussy approach worked well. Fears of the penalty if there was a repeat of the Elland Road brawl clearly had its impact on the players.

United gave one of their stereotypical stonewall performances, content to play on the counter and fifteen minutes from the end took the lead from a break. Madeley put O'Grady free on the edge of the penalty area with a 30-yard pass over the full-back. The Spanish defence clearly thought he was offside and pulled up, allowing the winger to pick his spot and fire low into the net.

It was Valencia's turn to be incensed.

There were scares after that for Leeds, but they hung on grimly for the 1-0 win that secured passage into the last eight.

Elland Road
Attendance: 34,414

Leeds United: Sprake, Reaney, Bell, Bremner, Charlton, Hunter, Storrie, Lorimer, Belfitt, Giles, O'Grady

Valencia: Nito, Arnal, Vidagany, Roberto, Mestre, Paquito, Guillot, Palau, Toto, Sanchez-Lage, Munoz

16

Tottenham Hotspur 3-1 Leeds United
First Division
20 August 1966

Three weeks after England lifted the World Cup, the snarling spirit of British football was captured perfectly in a photograph taken on the opening day of the League campaign. It was one of the most iconic of sporting images, featuring Spurs hard man Dave Mackay furiously hoisting a protesting Billy Bremner by his collar as referee Norman Burtenshaw raced up to avert the carnage.

After England's triumph, Don Revie had attempted to sign midfielder Alan Ball but missed out as the redhead opted for Everton, and he could have done with reinforcements to offset a growing injury list, which included Jack Charlton, Mike O'Grady, Alan Peacock and Albert Johanneson. However, for the game at Tottenham he could include Bobby Collins, making only his second first team appearance since suffering a fractured thigh almost a year earlier.

Tottenham had no such difficulties and included new signing Mike England in a team said to have cost £600,000, making it the most expensive selection ever in the Football League.

Tempers flared in the high temperatures as Mackay and Bremner clashed in midfield. Mackay: 'I fouled wee Billy and he got up and kicked me, so I lost my cool and grabbed hold of him. The truth is I was scared and I was bluffing my way out of the situation. I had just returned after an eighteen-month lay-off with a leg break, and when Billy kicked me it was like a warning that there were further reprisals on the way.'

Mackay had just returned to first team action after twice breaking the same leg. He had first sustained the fracture against Manchester United in December 1963; nine months later he made his comeback in a reserve team game with Shrewsbury and broke the leg again.

Mackay was understandably anxious and when Bremner kicked him on the self-same leg the red mist descended. He said:

[Bremner] was a brilliant little player but a dirty little b******. He kicked me in the leg I'd just come back from breaking twice. If he'd kicked the other one, I could have accepted that. But he kicked the broken one and that really annoyed me. I could've killed him that day.

Bremner replied:

> Dave Mackay thought I was going to have a go and he grabbed hold of me first. I was
> actually innocent. I had made my point and that was the end of it, but I think he believed
> that I was going to give him and everyone else a good kicking.

In modern times, both players would probably have been red carded, but back then
there were different standards, as Mackay noted: 'In the end the referee just gave us a
talking-to, for which I was relieved. I had got away with it and was so happy, because it
maintained my record of never having been sent off.'

When order was restored, United started to take control. Eric Stanger in the *Yorkshire
Post* commented:

> On the credit side there was the return to power of that remarkable little man, Bobby
> Collins, who not only came through his first severe test since breaking a thigh in Turin
> last October, but showed that there is still a lot of good football left in that small
> frame ... Only he knows how long and how hard was the fight, mental as well as
> physical, to come back. His reward came on Saturday.
>
> His courage was tested in an early heavy tackle with Mullery and not found
> wanting. In a shade temperature of 81 degrees, he trotted, ran and galloped non-stop,
> plugging a defensive hole here, scheming an opening there, saving his legs at times
> by his ability to read ahead the next two moves, and all the time driving and coaxing
> the others. His stamina and energy were astonishing and he outstayed players almost
> half his age.
>
> It was Collins who made the Leeds goal for Giles after 13 minutes, darting into an
> open space near the right corner flag to call for the ball to Lorimer and put over a
> centre of pinpoint accuracy. It was Collins who was desperately unlucky not to put
> Leeds level at 2-2 early in the second half when he brought the save of the match
> from Jennings from a free-kick and when the ball came back to him saw his crafty lob
> bounce off the bar.
>
> No doubt the heat had a lot to do with it for I never remember such a hot day for
> football. The wonder was that the standard of football was as high as it was and that
> there was only one bad incident involving lost temper.
>
> Tottenham, good in flashes but for a long time made to play the ball back or across
> the field because of the keen tackling and ready positioning of Bremner, Hunter and
> Madeley, a steady deputy for Charlton, got their first goal after 32 minutes. Then
> Mullery volleyed in from just outside the penalty area after an awkwardly bouncing
> ball had eluded three Leeds defenders.

Giles was replaced by Terry Cooper at half-time and United fell behind a minute later.
Cliff Jones centred from the left and Alan Gilzean just beat the onrushing Sprake to head
in off the post.

United rallied strongly, with Bremner leading their response. When he was fouled by
England on the edge of the Spurs box, Jennings was forced into a superb diving block by
a fearsomely driven free-kick from Collins and was reprieved when Collins' follow up
found the bar.

Spurs went further ahead after sixty-one minutes through Greaves, who five minutes later struck a post after being played in by Gilzean as United tottered. They had been destabilised by the loss of Giles and with Bremner pushed forward they didn't have the midfield platform from which to build.

In such sultry conditions, United found it impossible to pull back a two-goal deficit and at the end Venables fired against a post with Sprake beaten as Leeds were forced to give best on the day.

It was a disappointing start to United's campaign; they would quickly recover to launch their customary assault on all fronts and it was Bremner who led from the front, exuberantly filling the void as Collins' influence waned.

White Hart Lane
Attendance: 43,844

Tottenham Hotspur: Jennings, Beal, Knowles, Mullery, England, Mackay, Robertson, Greaves, Gilzean, Venables, Jones

Leeds United: Sprake, Reaney, Bell, Bremner, Madeley, Hunter, Lorimer, Collins, Belfitt, Giles (Cooper), Greenhoff

17

Valencia 0-2 Leeds United
Inter-Cities Fairs Cup: Third Round, Second Leg
8 February 1967

Coincidences crop up regularly in football and one such occurred when the Fairs Cup draw paired United with Valencia in a repeat of the tussle at the same stage of the competition twelve months previously.

When the draw was made for the 1967 tie, there was speculation about a potential bloodbath. The misgivings proved unfounded and there were just fifteen fouls in the first leg at Elland Road, eleven of them against the Spaniards. There were, however, a couple of torrid incidents in the game.

Keeper Pesudo was laid out after a frenetic United onslaught and five minutes' treatment was required before the referee could restart play. With the custodian refusing to get up, the Leeds crowd bayed with scorn. He was ultimately replaced by Abelardo.

The other clash came when Terry Cooper tried to hack the ball out of the new goalkeeper's hands. The Spaniards exacted retribution when Paquito scythed Cooper down.

By then, we had seen all the goals we were going to. Jimmy Greenhoff's scorcher from 15 yards gave United a twelve-minute lead, but it was nullified by Claramunt's effort after thirty-nine minutes.

United could never exploit their advantage and Don Revie conceded after the 1-1 draw that it would be difficult in Spain. The recently introduced away goals counting double rule meant that Leeds would need at least one score in Valencia to stand a chance of getting through.

The second leg looked daunting, given United's injury crisis. Paul Reaney was ruled out after a calf injury suffered days earlier at Everton and joined Jimmy Greenhoff, Mike O'Grady, Albert Johanneson, Terry Cooper, Alan Peacock and Rodney Johnson in the Elland Road treatment room.

Revie took a party of thirteen to Spain, omitting both Bobby Collins, in discussion with Bury about a prospective move, and Jim Storrie, who was also looking for a new club. The emphasis was on youth – seven players were twenty-one or less, including reserve keeper David Harvey. The only members of the party who had seen their twenty-seventh birthdays were Willie Bell and Jack Charlton.

Two days earlier, Billy Bremner had been told that he would shortly face a two-week suspension for being dismissed during a January match at Nottingham Forest. He was keen on making the most of the opportunity against Valencia.

Giles forced an unexpected breakthrough after seven minutes. The ball eluded Valencia left-back Tota near the halfway line and Giles was on it in an instant. He broke into space and, resisting challenges by Paquito, Mestre and Roberto, veered at pace towards the area. He coolly drew out keeper Pesudo before firing home an unstoppable left-footed drive.

It was the first time United had scored on their travels since Christmas Eve, and they nearly snatched a second goal moments later, but Belfitt was blocked as he made to shoot. The shock of the score provoked a forceful response and the Spaniards battered the Leeds rearguard, though United always threatened on the break.

Despite several scares, Leeds looked capable throughout an exhilarating match of getting the result they required. Valencia grew hasty in their approach play and increasingly ragged. Given confidence by their lead and cool ability to retain possession, United played poised football, always in control of the game, the axis of Bremner and Giles the constant pivot around which the display swung.

The Spanish forwards and midfielders were clearly frustrated; with Poli directing their play, Valencia tried everything they knew, but the English team made the clearer opportunities, even with so few men in advanced positions.

Three minutes from the end, United got the critical second goal that their display merited. Madeley's shot was blocked but Giles recovered it and fed Peter Lorimer, who fired home from close in.

That was the killer goal and sapped any remaining resistance. Valencia were devastated by the outcome, neutered by an English team at the peak of their powers; it was a thoroughly impressive exhibition of how to prosper in European football.

Acting captain Bremner said after the game:

> The Boss really won it for us, he hammered it into us day after day and time after time that we would win – not that we might win or could win but that we would win. The result was we went on the field really believing that we were the better side and we proved it … I was under his orders for no pessimism, and as I went on telling the lads we would win, I began to believe it ma'sel. It was wonderful and always will be with me, even if I play until a'm a hundred. We were absolutely convinced we could win when we went out.

Campo de Mestalla, Valencia
Attendance: 48,000

Valencia: Pesudo, Tatona, Tota, Paquito, Mestre, Roberto, Claramunt, Waldo, Ansola, Poli, Guillot

Leeds: Sprake, Madeley, Bell, Bremner, Charlton, Hunter, Giles, Lorimer, Belfitt, Gray, Hibbitt

18

England 2-3 Scotland
Home International Championship
15 April 1967

Don Revie's Leeds United owed much to the spirit and fight of the Scottish players with whom their ranks were swollen. National pride often spilled over into training sessions at Elland Road and few holds were barred when the Scots lined up against the Anglos, as recalled by Eddie Gray:

> Those five-a-side games could be brutal ... They were all-out war, even though everyone played for the same club. It didn't matter that Norman Hunter, Jack Charlton, Paul Madeley and Paul Reaney were Leeds teammates, only that they were English. Bobby Collins was the main instigator, but Billy [Bremner] played his part. Billy was usually not the best trainer, he never used to like any of the physical stuff. But once the ball came out and it was Scotland v England, it was like a switch had been flicked inside Billy. He became totally different. It was as if he was representing his country and winning was everything. The games eventually got so bad that Don had to stop them. He was worried someone would be seriously injured.

England's World Cup triumph in 1966 was more galling to Bremner and his compatriots than their country's own failure to qualify for the finals.

When the two sides met in April 1967, the English were still undefeated in the eight months since those finals, and Bremner and his colleagues were determined to end that run.

Though Scotland went into the game as underdogs, this was an era when they could boast some breathtaking talent; there was Bremner, of course, but the team also included four of the Celtic players who would beat Inter Milan to lift the European Cup a month later and two Rangers players who would feature in the Cup Winners Cup final. New manager Bobby Brown also had available to him the talents of Denis Law and Slim Jim Baxter, a sublime artist in midfield.

Scotland were brimming over with determination, though you wouldn't have known it from looking at Baxter before the game. As Brown delivered his first pre-match team talk, he was taken aback by the sight of Baxter flicking through the *Daily Telegraph*, and sought to put him in his place, asking, 'Anything to add, Jim?'

'Aye,' came the replay from Baxter. 'See this English lot, they can play nane.'

The silky Baxter would never play a greater game than he did that day, running the show on the wide-open planes of the Wembley pitch.

Bremner said,

I always remember one London newspaper writing 'I do not see it as being a repeat of the 1961 scoreline of 9-3. I cannot see the Scots scoring three goals.' That sort of reporting just made us all the more determined to do well.

There had been some nerves in the dressing room, but I will always remember Jim Baxter quietly telling us what he was going to do to humiliate this player or that player. We knew that he meant every word and he almost scared us.

As soon as the whistle blew to start the game we launched ourselves into the task. Jim Baxter did not waste any time in doing what he had said he was going to do. Once he had the ball, he challenged the English defenders to take it away from him and he was like a bullfighter, twisting this way and that with the ball firmly at his feet, as our opponents lunged to try to take it away. They found themselves tackling thin air as Jim pulled the ball out of reach or flicked it to one side at just the right moment.

He had said that he was going to take the mickey out of them and he certainly did. He was having the time of his life and he often just stood with one foot on the ball, daring them to come and take it.

After about ten minutes, Bobby Lennox for Scotland and Big Jack Charlton for England were both injured. Jack went off for about a quarter of an hour and then returned to take up a central attacking position. Later, the newspapers made the excuse that a few knocks had ruined the English game plan. They conveniently forgot to mention that Bobby Lennox carried his injury throughout the game and that Denis Law picked up an ankle injury before half-time that had him limping for the rest of the game.

Ironically we were down to ten men when the first goal came because Tommy Gemmell was stretched out behind the England goal having treatment when it was scored.

There was a tremendous roar when the ball hit the back of the net and anyone outside the stadium would have thought that England had scored, but it had been Denis Law who had set the game ablaze. Gordon Banks had saved his first effort, but Denis made no mistake with the rebound.

We should have rubbed in our advantage then, but we were content to continue playing good football rather than just go for goals. We wanted to show what we could do and Jim Baxter was trying to win a bet. In the dressing room before the game he had bet me how many times he could nutmeg various players. He really tormented the England defenders, so much so that I almost began to feel sorry for them.

England came at us in the second half, determined to stamp their authority on the game. Their pride had been hurt and they had been stung into action. We contained them, though. I sent a shot whistling past the post and then, from the goal kick, Alan Ball picked up the ball and sent it to Bobby Charlton who let fly with a shot that Ronnie Simpson could only block. The ball went high into the air and when it came down, Charlton headed it towards the goal. Ronnie Simpson dropped on it on the line and there were English protests that the ball had crossed the goal line. I was right on the spot and it definitely did not, although I would hardly expect any England supporter to believe me.

The Tartan Army went even crazier when we went 2-0 ahead thanks to a Bobby Lennox goal with just under a quarter of an hour left. England became really desperate then and I remember Alan Ball shouting so much that his voice went even higher than usual and nobody could understand a word that he was saying.

Five minutes from the end there was a bit of confusion and Jack Charlton ended a move by scoring. We got going again and Denis Law tried a chip which had 'world-class goal' written all over it. However, a world-class save from Gordon Banks stopped it. Jim McCalliog was not to be outdone, though, and a bit of fancy footwork between him and Bobby Lennox ended with Jim putting us 3-1 ahead.

There was just time for Geoff Hurst to make it 3-2 and that was how it stayed until the end of the game. We had won a sensational victory and the Tartan Army were having their biggest and best party for years. The Wembley pitch was completely covered by dancing Scottish fans. I was dancing with them.

When we got back to the dressing room, Jim Baxter worked out how much he had won on his various bets.

It came home to all of us that England were world champions and we were the first team to beat them since they had won the World Cup, and that made us the new world champions as far as we concerned. Nobody was going to take that moment of glory away from us and they never have.

Wembley Stadium
Attendance: 99,063

England: Banks, Cohen, Wilson, Stiles, J. Charlton, Moore, Ball, Greaves, R. Charlton, Hurst, Peters

Scotland: Simpson, Gemmell, McCreadie, Greig, McKinnon, Bremner, McCalliog, Law, Wallace, Baxter, Lennox

19

Leeds United 0-1 Chelsea
FA Cup Semi-Final
29 April 1967

For the second time in three seasons, Leeds United had reached the last four of the FA Cup where they faced Chelsea, offering the chance of retribution for an undeserved fourth round defeat in 1966.

Don Revie took a squad of thirteen to prepare at a Midlands hotel in the week before the game, recuperating after a spell of thirteen matches in forty-three days, as they chased an unlikely treble of League championship, Cup and Fairs Cup. Albert Johanneson was left behind in Leeds after suffering an injury in training and Jack Charlton was unavailable with a broken toe suffered on England duty, though he travelled with the squad; Paul Madeley filled the centre half vacancy.

Chelsea could select from strength with Tony Hateley, for many weeks earlier in the campaign a transfer target for Revie, leading the attack.

On a warm afternoon, 62,378 fans packed into Villa Park, providing receipts of £32,490, a record for the stadium outside of World Cup games. The two sets of fans cheerfully goaded each other across the packed terraces.

The Londoners were quickly into their stride and had the better of the first thirty minutes, with Charlie Cooke's movement and trickery giving United some uneasy moments. He was the most penetrative forward on a day of defensive dominance.

Chelsea were unlucky not to be awarded a penalty after seven minutes when Gary Sprake's extended boot ended in Boyle's face as the two jumped for a ball.

The game was played for the most part in the Leeds half and United's thrusts were few and far between. Eddie Gray, Terry Cooper and Billy Bremner had some decent efforts but could develop no momentum.

Bremner was constantly in the action, and figured prominently at both ends of the park. Guarding the post at one corner, he had little option but to turn a John Hollins effort behind for another flag kick. Later, the Scot was going through on the Chelsea goal when Eddie McCreadie fouled him.

It was a brutal first half and looked set to end in deadlock, but with moments to go the Londoners took the lead.

Eric Stanger in the *Yorkshire Post* commented:

It was a magnificent effort in the last minute of the first half made out of a trifle by Cooke, Chelsea's best forward ... He slipped past Bremner and Belfitt on the left touchline, took a return pass from McCreadie and belted over a centre to Hateley as hard as he could. A more orthodox, floated centre and Hateley could never have got the power behind his header as he did to beat Sprake. Hateley paid a lot off his £100,000 fee with that effort.

It was a decent goal, with Hateley for once managing to evade the grim clutches of his marker. Madeley had played well but was not as strong in the air as Charlton. Having got the run on the centre half, Hateley converted the chance smartly.

After the break, United threw Bremner up front, with Gray dropping deeper to fill the void. Though Cooke and Chelsea continued to carve out openings, Bremner's presence made Leeds more threatening and there were several chances, with Bonetti in constant action.

The heat of the contest rose as crunching tackles flew in, and Greenhoff had to come off for attention on the hour. Ten minutes later, Belfitt was withdrawn after another clash left him injured; Peter Lorimer came on to offer fresh legs to United's cause. He had an immediate impact and Leeds started posing some difficult questions.

A head of steam was being built up as United camped in the Chelsea half, though they struggled to manufacture a clear opening. With seven minutes to go, it looked like Leeds would finally fashion an equaliser.

From a long Greenhoff punt to the edge of the area, Bremner nodded through Chelsea's square back line. Terry Cooper strode onto the ball and thrashed it home. As Leeds began to celebrate, referee Ken Burns ruled Cooper offside and the goal void. Bremner was unconvinced, maintaining, 'Terry was definitely lying onside when I flicked the ball on to him.'

United rallied and pressed Chelsea into some untidy defensive work. Paul Reaney broke forward to shoot, and a scramble in the Londoners area ended with a Leeds throw on the left. After receiving the ball 25 yards out, Norman Hunter was pulled back by Bobby Tambling and the referee awarded a free-kick. He marched the Chelsea wall back the required 10 yards. Johnny Giles took what he considered the signal from the official to proceed and rolled the ball sideways to the waiting Lorimer, who slammed the ball unerringly into the Chelsea net.

The Leeds players leapt in the air with joy while the Londoners hung their heads in despair, but pandemonium broke out as Ken Burns signalled for the kick to be retaken. He ruled that the wall had encroached, his fastidiousness denying the offended team an advantage. The decision sparked mass protests and violent argument, but Burns would brook no debate. What was even more exasperating was that he seemed to wait until the ball had entered the net before signalling that there was a problem.

Johnny Giles said,

The referee came back to me from shifting the Chelsea players to the 10-yard mark and we looked at each other. Now I have taken dozens of free-kicks just on an exchange of looks with the referee. It's accepted. I'll admit he made no signal or sound, but he could see I was wanting to take the kick, and he looked at me. So I took it. Chelsea were still encroaching, but the advantage was with us in taking the kick.

It was so long that Peter had twice shouted to me to roll the ball to him. Each time I said: 'Quiet, if Chelsea hear they'll pull a man out to block the shot,' for they were obviously expecting me to chip the ball to the far post. Then the referee turned from the Chelsea players to face me. I thought it was in order to take the free-kick and slipped the ball across to Peter. I was dumbfounded when he ordered the kick to be retaken.

Inevitably, the retaken kick came to nothing and Chelsea survived the onslaught. Seconds later, Burns whistled for full time and the distraught Leeds party collapsed in anguish. They had been cruelly denied by refereeing decisions, a recurring theme of their years under Don Revie.

Still, who were United to argue? In the fifth round against Sunderland the same Ken Burns had awarded them a dubious late penalty. But the Leeds United perspective, like that of most teams, has always been one-eyed.

United's FA Cup campaign was over for another year.

Villa Park
Attendance: 62,378

Leeds United: Sprake, Reaney, Bell, Bremner, Madeley, Hunter, Giles, Belfitt (Lorimer), Greenhoff, Gray, Cooper

Chelsea: Bonetti, A. Harris, McCreadie, Hollins, Hinton, R. Harris, Cooke, Baldwin, Hateley, Tambling, Boyle

20

Leeds United 7-0 Chelsea
First Division
7 October 1967

Leeds United have built up several keen rivalries over the years. By 1967, Chelsea were fixtures on the list. The Blues had been United's nemesis in the FA Cup in each of the previous two years and the First Division encounter between the two teams at Elland Road in October 1967 was inevitably seen by Leeds as a chance for revenge. Their opponents arrived in disarray following the resignation of manager Tommy Docherty the day before the game.

The Guardian wrote:

> [Docherty] resigned a few hours after he had received a 28-day suspension from all football activity following incidents on the club's goodwill tour of Bermuda in June. The resignation takes immediate effect and Docherty did not travel to Leeds.
>
> In Bermuda Docherty had criticised referees and the arrangements of the tour, in which two players were sent off ... Docherty said yesterday: 'I had no chance to defend myself in public, and would have asked for a personal hearing.' When the report arrived from Bermuda he gave the FA his version of the incidents. He thought the incidents had been dealt with and forgotten.
>
> Docherty cannot have any part of football for a month, and cannot draw any of his salary of £7,000 a year in the month – a loss of nearly £600. He will be, said Dennis Follows, secretary of the FA, completely divorced from the game. It means that he may not pay to watch football from the terraces.

Chelsea were nineteenth, without a win in a month. In sharp contrast, United were unbeaten since 30 August. They had conceded only five goals in the nine games since then and were facing Chelsea just four days after beating Spora of Luxembourg 9-0.

The only cloud on the horizon was Billy Bremner's twenty-eight-day suspension. He received the ban for his dismissal in a match at Fulham in September. It brought the Scot's disciplinary sanctions over recent years to sixty-eight-days' suspension and £350 in fines. The Chelsea game was Bremner's last appearance before his exclusion and he was determined to sign off with a bang.

The affair was something of a watershed, as Bremner recounted in *You Get Nowt For Being Second*:

> I believe the turning point for Billy Bremner came in a game against Fulham. Mark Pearson and myself clashed, but it was a relatively minor affair, and called for only a

few quiet words from the referee. In short, it was a simple order to 'tone it down, lads', and sensibly Mark accepted the admonition and kept his counsel.

But not Billy Bremner. Oh no. I had got it into my nut that I had not been at fault in any shape or form and I was determined that the referee, if not the whole world, should know this. So I kept on going, full steam ahead, arguing the toss with the ref. And instead of the ticking off which should have been the end of the affair, Billy Bremner's name went into the black book, as my big mouth got the better of me.

Even that didn't satisfy me or quieten me down. For even after play had restarted, I couldn't keep my mouth closed and I carried on the verbal feuding. I was so righteously indignant that I couldn't even see the danger signals. And in the end, I was given my marching orders and sent for an early bath. It was a fate which I fully deserved.

As I was getting stripped and changed in the lonely dressing room, while the muted roar of the crowd sounded from a distance, I kept telling myself fiercely what an idiot I'd been. Me and my big mouth. Why COULDN'T I have had the sense to keep quiet, like Mark Pearson? I laid it on thick and heavy to myself, but that was nothing to what I got from Don Revie when we came face to face. What he called me cannot be repeated, but I can tell you that he got it all off his chest. And every word flew straight in my direction.

Don Revie let me know, in no uncertain fashion, that I was letting myself down by such unseemly outbursts. Not only that, but even more important, I was letting my teammates down. And in his book, letting the side down in professional football is the cardinal sin.

So, at long last, I realised that trouble and I MUST part company if I were to do myself and Leeds United full justice.

Bremner took out his frustration on Chelsea in a game long remembered for his display.

The returning Albert Johanneson broke the deadlock after five minutes. The goal ensured that any brittle confidence remaining after Docherty's departure would come under the severest of examinations.

After eleven minutes, Jimmy Greenhoff made it 2-0 with a fierce drive and then Jack Charlton headed home a third in the fourteenth minute after Eddie Gray's inswinging corner had been misjudged by Bonetti – Chelsea were shell shocked by the United onslaught.

There was a lull in affairs for the next twenty minutes as United drew breath but they went four ahead six minutes before the break when Lorimer's fierce shot from the angle beat Bonetti.

The game was over as a contest and Leeds could operate on autopilot after the interval. Gray beat Bonetti with a magnificent shot from the edge of the penalty area on the hour to keep the score sheet ticking over, but United were now content to play the game at half pace.

With ten minutes to go, Chelsea defender Marvin Hinton had the misfortune to see another Lorimer power drive deflect off him past Bonetti, but that was a mere appetiser for the coup de grace.

Eric Stanger said:

The man of the match was unquestionably Bremner, who chose this final appearance to give a virtuoso performance. To Chelsea's credit, however much Bremner teased and tormented them with his astonishing dexterity of foot and his remarkable sense of balance, so that he could turn and twist on the proverbial sixpence, they never tried to ruffle his temper. Nor, on his part was Bremner guilty of one foul tackle.

It was a great demonstration of attacking wing-half play by any standards and, having made the first two goals (with considerable help from Reaney) and the fourth for Lorimer, Bremner bowed himself out of football for a time with a fine sense of the dramatic.

Eight minutes from the end he got the last goal from Jones' forward header with a spectacular bicycle kick, so beloved by Continentals and South Americans. It brought down the house of 40,460 as it deserved to do.

Phil Brown wrote in the *Evening Post*:

Billy Bremner departed into the seclusion of suspension after playing one of the greatest games of his young life. Even if Chelsea could have offered rather more resistance at Elland Road against Leeds United than they did, he nevertheless reached the football heights.

He showed just what a vintage champagne footballer he can be. His passes flowed like pieces of silk unrolling, prompting the taker into an opening perfectly, and his reverse pass, the best in the industry for me, and given to very few of my time, flashed several times to cut out a third of the defence. Nor did he commit one foul or utter one offending word.

It was, I suppose, only in the script that he should score the goal of the game, taking it with a perfect specimen of the falling overhead shot, commonly known as the bicycle kick. A final stroke by an artist on a masterpiece, as it were.

Elland Road
Attendance: 40,460

Leeds United: Sprake, Reaney, Madeley, Bremner, Charlton, Hunter, Greenhoff, Lorimer, Jones (Hibbitt), Gray, Johanneson

Chelsea: Bonetti, Thomson, Hinton, Harris, Butler, Hollins, Boyle, Cooke, Osgood, Baldwin, McCreadie

21

Arsenal 0-1 Leeds United
Football League Cup Final
2 March 1968

As Leeds prepared for their Football League Cup final against Arsenal, there were two schools of thought regarding the outcome. The Doubting Thomases looked back on two lost finals, a couple of League runners up spots and two defeats in semi-finals, and concluded that Leeds were bottlers, prone to freeze on the big occasion.

United proponents pointed to their status as the team of the season, still in the running for four trophies and on a sixteen-game unbeaten run that incorporated eight clean sheets.

Billy Bremner oozed assurance, saying, 'The boys are all very confident of winning this one. We only hope we do not suffer from over-confidence.'

Leeds were eager to wipe out the memory of their previous appearance at Wembley, the sterile 1965 FA Cup final, but the priority was victory and an end to the hard luck stories.

The League Cup's status of being the least significant of the major trophies mattered little to Leeds – a trophy was a trophy.

Leeds had injury and illness concerns ahead of the big day, but could name Jack Charlton (back problems), Gary Sprake, Jimmy Greenhoff (both knee strains) and Johnny Giles (chill) in their starting eleven, though the last two were far from fully fit. It was a gamble that Revie felt worth taking, for Giles had enjoyed a wonderful season and was the man who made United tick. Cup-tied Mick Jones was replaced at centre forward by Paul Madeley.

Billy Bremner, now firmly established as captain after the departure of Bobby Collins and the abdication of Jack Charlton, led his men out determined to put on a show worthy of the occasion.

United took the game to the Gunners in the opening minutes, with Bob McNab having to intercept a neat through pass from Bremner to Madeley, and then Eddie Gray probing up the left flank. Arsenal responded smartly to create a decent opening but young David Jenkins sent it high, wide and not particularly handsome.

There were several long balls played high into the penalty areas, but the defensive kingpins, Charlton and Ian Ure, gobbled up everything that came their way.

The Gunners were starting to make their mark, but it was United who broke through after eighteen minutes.

Bremner went away down the right to win a corner. The ball found Giles, whose shot was deflected to bring another flag kick, and this time Gray's centre was more dangerous, dropping perfectly to the heart of a crowded goal area. With both Madeley and Charlton to contend with, Gunners keeper Jim Furnell flapped desperately at the ball, sending it out aimlessly to the left-hand side of the penalty area, where Terry Cooper was waiting. The full-back moved in eagerly to volley it unerringly back into the corner from whence it came.

Arsenal protested long and hard that Furnell had been impeded, but referee Hamer would have none of it.

Arsenal were visibly shaken and Ure nearly laid a chance on a plate for Greenhoff with a tentative pass back to his keeper, but the Gunners recovered thereafter and came out to pressurise United.

Frustrated by an inability to convert their dominance into clear openings, Arsenal tried to turn United's own dead ball tactics against them at a corner shortly before the break. McLintock heavily charged Sprake as he caught the cross, sparking an untidy set to. Ure was surrounded by Leeds defenders pushing and pulling him in concerted rage. The referee calmed affairs quickly, though things had threatened to get out of hand. It was just as well that the half-time whistle went shortly afterwards to give time for tempers to cool.

The Whites came out of their shell for a moment when Paul Reaney's speedy overlap took him clear to set up a break which ended with Bremner's blazing shot flying across the goal and wide of the far post.

Later, the Leeds skipper chased a loose ball into the box and nearly took Furnell's head off his shoulders in his eagerness to get in a shot, provoking more anger in the Gunners ranks.

Such chances were becoming scarcer as United settled into a containing game. They had missed too many opportunities of success to throw this one away now. Madeley was withdrawn into an auxiliary defensive role, with Rod Belfitt coming on for a limping Gray with fifteen minutes to go to plough a lone forward furrow.

Sprake had to make one late save, diving low to his left to turn a good shot from Radford away for a corner, but, that apart, Arsenal had few direct chances. They did get the ball in the net once, but Geordie Armstrong's effort was disallowed for an infringement on Giles.

The stars on the day were all in defence and few played better than Hunter and Cooper, faultless in their covering and tackling, and ever ready to spring counters.

The splendid Leeds defence held out to register its fifth clean sheet in nine matches; the match was hardly thrilling, but it was a job well done.

Eric Stanger in the *Yorkshire Post* wrote:

Leeds played the more thoughtful football but they were caught in possession in midfield far more than usual, partly because of the sharpness of Arsenal to get to the ball and partly because their passes were not always made quickly enough. Giles played under difficulty for he had not thrown off the effects of his heavy cold and did well to finish the match. In the circumstances, it was not surprising to see him less effective than usual.

Bremner, the other half of the link, led his men with such courage and determination that in the last 20 minutes when Leeds were battling away for dear life as Arsenal strove desperately to snatch an equaliser he was prepared to take on the whole Arsenal side if necessary. One hand was already on the Cup and while Bremner had breath no one was going to wrest it from him.

It was a drab and dull game for the neutrals, but no one at Elland Road were overly bothered. Harry Reynolds' desperate desire to 'win summat' was the only driving force that United cared about, and few could deny that they deserved their moment of glory.

Wembley Stadium
Attendance: 97,887

Arsenal: Furnell, Storey, McNab, McLintock, Simpson, Ure, Radford, Jenkins (Neill), Graham, Sammels, Armstrong

Leeds United: Sprake, Reaney, Cooper, Bremner, Charlton, Hunter, Greenhoff, Lorimer, Madeley, Giles, Gray (Belfitt)

22

Leeds United 1-0 Ferencvaros
Fairs Cup Final, First Leg
7 August 1968

Since making their bow in 1965, Leeds United had established an impressive track record in the Fairs Cup. At their first attempt, they reached the semi-finals and a year later lost to Dinamo Zagreb in the final.

United made it down to the last two once more in 1968, pitted against the crack Hungarian outfit Ferencvaros, reckoned by both Sir Matt Busby and Bill Shankly to be the best side in Europe. Their star man was twenty-seven-year-old striker Florian Albert, who shone in the 1966 World Cup finals, when he single-handedly devastated world champions Brazil with a hat-trick; he was crowned European Footballer of the Year a year later.

The final was held over to the start of the 1968/69 season because of fixture congestion and United warmed up for the first leg with a friendly against Celtic. A 2-1 victory boosted the Whites and their mood was further improved by enhancements to their Elland Road stadium, as noted by Eric Todd in *The Guardian*: 'With a splendid new stand at the Lowfields Road end, two new ultra-modern floodlighting pylons to keep it company, and the pitch in beautiful condition, the ground at last looked like a place fit for heroes to watch in.'

Richard Ulyatt said in the *Yorkshire Post*:

Leeds, without a true winger in the team, had the greatest difficulty in outflanking the first line of three defenders Ferencvaros fielded and seldom managed to get round the second line of four players. When they did so, Gray, in particular, and Lorimer were so slow that the initiative was quickly lost. A good old fashioned winger might have been in his element against a defence that was by no means on top form.

As Leeds interpreted it, free expression, their much-vaunted new policy, seemed to be largely the mixture as before, with Charlton, Bremner, Hunter and Cooper slightly more frequently on attack, and Madeley dropping back as a second centre half, the sort of thing we saw time after time last season. There was no increased effort by the forwards in the face of keen and sometimes ruthless spoiling, except perhaps from Jones, who was much more like a £100,000 player than during last season.

The Hungarians had the first chance, Charlton's hesitation on the edge of his area conceding possession to Albert. He found Szoke but the opportunity was wasted as the shot flew wide.

United fought back and came close to a score shortly afterwards. Ferencvaros keeper Geczi was awarded a free-kick virtually under his own bar, but his kick was poor and the ball fell to Jones, loitering with intent on the edge of the box. He instantly fed Lorimer, who slammed in a ferocious shot. Geczi made up for his error by making a wonderful save at the expense of a corner.

United had identified the Hungarian keeper as a potential weakness, as Johnny Giles recalled:

> They might well have gained the stalemate they wanted ... but for the glaring vulnerability of their goalkeeper Geczi in dealing with crosses. We remembered that, during the World Cup, Hungary's goalkeeper had great difficulty in catching these high balls and, in fact, many people consider that had Hungary possessed a keeper of the calibre of Gordon Banks they would have got through to the final against England. During the early stages we set out to test Geczi's ability in this particular department and it didn't take us long to find out that he, too, was ill at ease when the ball was flighted into his goalmouth.
>
> From one cross earlier on he dropped the ball straight to the feet of Norman Hunter, ten yards out, but the wing-half was so surprised at his good fortune that he mishit his shot and was well off target. Geczi lost his nerve and I cannot recall him holding one cross ball all evening!

Leeds had the better of things as the Hungarians let them pass the ball around at leisure while out of shooting range. Though United penned Ferencvaros back for long periods, they usually had to settle for corners and it was the visitors who exhibited the better shooting when opportunities presented themselves. In one move, Albert and Varga got the better of Giles and Madeley in midfield to free Fenyvesi. He centred for Szoke but the chance was lost when the forward tried to shift the ball onto his right foot before shooting.

After forty-one minutes, however, the United pressure paid off. When Jones forced a corner, United, renowned for their dead ball routines, gleefully capitalised.

Giles: 'As Jack Charlton took up his familiar position on the goal line, the Hungarian defenders surrounded him in an effort to protect Geczi. But they succeeded only in making his job a lot more difficult. As the ball came across from Peter Lorimer, there were so many bodies in the goalmouth that Geczi could only get his fingertips to it. The ball broke loose from the ruck, and there was Jones on the spot to add the finishing touch.'

Leeds started the second half with intricate passing rather than using the wind that was now in their favour. On too many occasions they ran the ball into the massed ranks of Hungarian defenders, with centre back Juhasz an obdurate barrier.

After sixty-five minutes, both teams made a change. Ferencvaros brought on Balint for Fenyvesi, while Giles had to go off with double vision; he was replaced by Jimmy Greenhoff, who was quickly into the action with a header on goal.

Five minutes later, Leeds had to use their second sub, as reported by Eric Todd in *The Guardian*:

> There was serious trouble on the field for the first time. Jones was going through and as he entered the penalty area, Geczi advanced and threw himself ... at the Leeds

centre forward. If this had been a rugby match, Leeds would almost certainly have been awarded a penalty try. It transpired, however, that the whistle had been blown before Jones embarked on his solo run so that no goal and no penalty would have been allowed in any case. Nevertheless, it was a shocking foul which merited some sort of punishment. Geczi, applauded so many times previously, now was jeered repeatedly while the hapless Jones was removed on a stretcher and his place was taken by Belfitt.

Those changes disrupted United's rhythm and allowed the Hungarians to come into the game, Charlton doing well to rob Varga on the point of shooting. Later, Rakosi was foiled by a brilliant save from Sprake, when he looked to have an easy chance, but Ferencvaros could not turn their sudden flurry of activity into goals and had to reconcile themselves to a one-goal deficit

The game was no thriller, but United had secured a considerable victory. With Billy Bremner ('industry exemplified,' according to Eric Todd) making his normal dynamic contribution, Leeds fully merited their advantage. The Scot was everywhere, leading from the front, determined that there should be no mistake. He was now a mature twenty-five-year-old, comfortable with the mantle of captain, but still with enough fire in his belly to ensure Leeds would never be outfought. Johnny Giles was the playmaker, the fulcrum, the brains of the team, but Bremner was the heartbeat, the spirit and the passion.

Elland Road
Attendance: 25,268

Leeds United: Sprake, Reaney, Cooper, Bremner, Charlton, Hunter, Lorimer, Madeley, Jones (Belfitt), Giles (Greenhoff), Gray

Ferencvaros: Geczi, Novak, Pancsics, Havasi, Juhasz, Szucs, Szoke, Varga, Albert, Rakosi, Fenyvesi (Balint)

23

Ferencvaros 0-0 Leeds United
Fairs Cup Final, Second Leg
11 September 1968

11 September 1968 brought a moment of truth as Leeds United faced mighty Ferencvaros of Budapest in the second leg of the Inter-Cities Fairs Cup final enjoying the advantage of a 1-0 first leg victory. They were desperate to become the first British team to win the trophy and prove their many critics wrong.

Those who were not fully converted to the Leeds cause believed the Hungarians' world-class attack would be too strong for United. There had been enough flashes in the first leg to leave little doubt as to the threat Florian Albert and his men represented.

With Johnny Giles and Eddie Gray unavailable through injury, and Jimmy Greenhoff now at Birmingham, Don Revie drafted Mike O'Grady and Terry Hibbitt into his line up. They would be useful outlets, while Terry Cooper's sorties down the left were becoming a key part of United's offensive armoury. Nevertheless, Revie's tactics were founded on a smothering defensive barrier across midfield, for the most part leaving Mick Jones alone up front. It was a tactic honed into second nature over three hard years of Fairs Cup competition.

The Nep Stadium was a magnificent venue for a historic occasion, and Billy Bremner led out his men determined not to yield an inch.

Ferencvaros were straight onto the attack, and committed themselves to all-out assaults on Gary Sprake's goal. Whether by design or not, United dropped into defence, packing their box and funnelling back behind the ball. For all that, the Hungarians struggled to pose any direct threat and it was sixteen minutes before a real goal attempt was made, so tight was the United covering.

Bremner said:

80,000 Hungarian supporters watched as Ferencvaros mounted attack after attack, and Leeds pulled out all the defensive stops. Players like Terry Cooper, Norman Hunter and Paul Madeley played like two men, Gary Sprake never made a slip in goal, and Jack Charlton used his head to superb effect in nodding away the ball which Ferencvaros persisted in thumping down the field.

Albert and Varga of Ferencvaros certainly did their best to prise open the Leeds defence, but they couldn't manage it on their own. The Hungarian attack, too, didn't really click as a unit. A lot of the scoring attempts came from individual attempts to break through, or from chasing a long ball booted down the middle.

Right from the kick-off, Ferencvaros left us in no doubt that they intended to bank on all-out attack. In turn, we left them in no doubt at all that they were up against a bunch of unyielding Yorkshiremen. We packed our defence so solidly that it was a full twenty minutes before any real threat approached our goal. Rakosi got through to our penalty area, which was packed with white shirts, and let loose a flyer. He was wasting his time – Terry Cooper made it all look so easy when he cleared the ball with a seemingly casual overhead kick. I have to say that I breathed a little more easily when I saw that Terry's move had been successful, I can tell you!

A few minutes later it was Terry to the rescue again. He deflected a low, hard shot from Albert and eased the pressure once again.

During the opening twenty minutes, United oozed calm confidence, taking pains to retain what little possession they had. The green-shirted Hungarians swarmed all round them, but cool heads were everywhere. There were no panicky clearances and United grew in assurance. They broke out in the thirty-fifth minute to earn a free-kick wide on the right, giving Jack Charlton the opportunity to make one of his customary advances. The Hungarians had seen enough of the defender's aerial dominance in the first leg to know the threat he offered at dead ball situations.

With the attention focused on Charlton, Jones was given the space to meet O'Grady's free-kick and his high looping header dropped onto the bar before going behind. It was a clear demonstration that Ferencvaros dare not take Leeds lightly, with O'Grady probing dangerously down both wings. Two more shots followed in quick succession, though keeper Geczi parried them both.

These were rare moments of relief as United were forced to defend in depth, with most the game played in their defensive third, and Albert and Varga conspicuous in attack. Nevertheless, Leeds had found the measure of the Ferencvaros forwards, reading their intention almost before they made their move. The front line were among the world's best, but had encountered nothing like this resolute defence. Even with Novak and Szoke controlling the right flank and Varga and Rakosi the other, giving defender Juhasz the opportunity to join in, Ferencvaros could find no way through or around a white wall.

Bremner commented:

As soon as the whistle had gone to signal the start of the second half, we were thrown back once more, as right winger Szoke hared down the line and whipped in an angled shot to which Gary Sprake leaped for a brilliant save. Then we were caught out when one of the Ferencvaros forwards slipped into our penalty area, kept on running, but made a smart back-pass for a teammate to collect. For a few seconds, we really were all at sea, but the danger was soon over – the shot went harmlessly wide.

Rakosi sent in a first time shot from a high Varga centre, but again the shot was wide. Sprake had to save with his feet from Szoke, making one of his final contributions. The Ferencvaros attacks were like a wave and on the hour they sought to give themselves fresh impetus, bringing on Karaba to replace him. Eight minutes later, Don Revie made a tactical switch, replacing the tiring Hibbitt with Mick Bates as the Hungarians continued to press.

Now Ferencvaros found a second wind and intensified their efforts to snatch an equaliser, forcing a succession of corners and hemming United into their own box.

Most of the chances that had fallen to Ferencvaros had gone to Rakosi, but he was found wanting when they arose. As the game entered its final ten minutes, the Ferencvaros attacks grew more intense, with thrusts coming from everywhere.

In the eighty-sixth minute, the Nep rose as one as Varga cut in from the left to beat Sprake, but United were reprieved when West German referee Schulenberg ruled the effort offside. Then Bremner had to clear from Albert, Varga's overhead strike just beat the post and Sprake was forced to dive at Albert's feet to deny him a shot.

Geoffrey Green said in *The Times*:

> In the second half Leeds were camped in their own half as the Hungarians threw all their efforts into trying to make the breakthrough. But Leeds held their lines superbly and twice were saved by dazzling saves by Sprake under his crossbar. First he kept out a close-range effort from Szoke with his left foot, and then he dived with poetic grace to turn away a free-kick from the edge of the penalty area to his top corner from Novak. How the goalkeeper ever saw the ball at that moment was miraculous, since there was a solid wall of ten white shirts in front of him.

The save from Novak was the finest moment of Gary Sprake's footballing career and it signified almost symbolically that Ferencvaros' challenge was exhausted. They had thrown everything they could at United's stonewall defence for ninety enthralling minutes and had been resolutely defied.

They had given the United defence a stern test, with inside right Varga trying everything he knew to work his way through the eye of a needle. He never stood a chance against a team that was peerless in the defensive arts.

The final whistle went and the neon-lit scoreboard said it all – Ferencvaros 0 Leeds United 0 – the Inter-Cities Fairs Cup was won.

Billy Bremner went up to receive the trophy from Sir Stanley Rous, president of FIFA, and the United players embarked on a lap of honour to mark a historic victory, greeted with triumph in the British press.

Desmond Hackett (*Express*) said, 'When tired limbs screamed rebellion over extra exertion, there was not one Leeds player who failed to drive himself in that further yard of effort.'

He didn't say so, but Revie knew that the victory would come as a real slap in the face for United's many critics, those who had written so spitefully following the dull-as-dishwater League Cup final victory over Arsenal and had not even tried to hide their pleasure when Everton beat Leeds in the FA Cup semi-final.

Bremner said:

> It was a moment to savour. For ten years one British team after another had been trying vainly to win this competition. It had always been looked upon as the toughest competition of them all in many ways, because the tournament seemed to spark off trouble and strife of one kind or another nearly every season. British clubs had travelled all over Europe in their efforts to lift this trophy and now, at last, it was Leeds United who had done it.

We were called a defensive-minded team – and I'm sure that there has been some justification for being so labelled at times in the past. However, on that night we did no more than any other British team would have done. We played it really tight at the back ... I admit it was a defensive display, but it was a superb one and it was successful!

Nep Stadium, Budapest
Attendance: 76,000

Ferencvaros: Geczi, Novak, Pancsics, Havasi, Juhasz, Szucs, Rakosi, Szoke (Karaba), Varga, Albert, Katona

Leeds: Sprake, Reaney, Cooper, Bremner, Charlton, Hunter, O'Grady, Lorimer, Jones, Madeley, Hibbitt (Bates)

24

Liverpool 0-0 Leeds United
First Division
28 April 1969

April 1969: Don Revie had spent eight eventful years building Leeds United into a team that could challenge for the game's honours and they now had the chance to cement their standing as they faced Liverpool in a League championship showdown.

The match had originally been scheduled for 22 March, but a twist of fate saw to it that the top two sides would meet at Anfield as the season reached its final knockings. The original fixture was postponed because of a flu epidemic at Elland Road.

The decision to defer was a controversial one, particularly as United had also previously been given leave to bring forward some of their Easter fixtures. Liverpool were furious at the news, hinting darkly at conspiracy.

At the time of the original scheduling, Liverpool lagged six points behind United with a game in hand, and their title challenge was being frustrated by the weather. They had played just once in a month and being forced to kick their heels while Leeds won three straight games, gifting the momentum to the Whites.

By the time the rearranged fixture came around, Leeds' lead was five points. United had only Liverpool and Nottingham Forest to face, while the Reds had three games left.

The title rivals each played out goalless draws away from home on 22 April, United defying third-placed Everton at Goodison while Liverpool surprisingly dropped a point at relegation-threatened Coventry. Those results left the advantage with Leeds. A point at Anfield would guarantee the title; if Liverpool were victorious, then United could still secure the title by beating Forest at home two days later.

Leeds went into the game in marginally the better form – they were undefeated in the League since losing 5-1 at Burnley in October, and had conceded just two goals in the previous seven games. Liverpool themselves had not lost since 15 February, but had been involved in too many draws. The points difference had remained stubbornly at four or more for eight weeks.

Revie could select from strength; his only change from the Everton game was the recall of the fit again Mick Jones, with Peter Lorimer dropping to the bench.

Liverpool were unchanged, though this meant they would continue without World Cup winner Roger Hunt, who had not played since dislocating a collarbone at Stoke on Easter Monday, two days after he scored his 300th goal for the Reds. Alun Evans, who became Britain's first £100,000 teenager when he arrived from Wolves earlier in the season, would continue to lead the attack.

Revie promised that United would attack whenever they had the chance. Few who had seen them play over the previous five years gave much credence to those claims and it was clear from the off that Leeds would be content with a clean sheet.

There were 53,750 passionate football followers in the stadium, but hundreds more were locked outside when the gates were closed five minutes before the off.

Billy Bremner won the toss and chose to make Liverpool play towards the Kop in the first half. It was a calculated risk, leaving Leeds to weather a fearsome opening burst. As Bremner later told Phil Brown of the *Yorkshire Evening Post*, 'The team was unusually nervous when it went out. I have never known them like they were tonight. It was worse than our FA Cup final. I was nervous. I couldn't sleep the night before, and that isn't me. I even got up out of bed at four o'clock in the morning and smoked a cigarette to try and stop thinking about the game.'

Sure enough, the opening was frenetic. At first, United could not hide their anxiety, rushing everything they did and making some rash challenges. Liverpool were just as wound up by the occasion, and there were some fierce opening exchanges. United committed two fouls in five minutes and Liverpool retorted with four in five, all six driven by nerves. In that period Tommy Smith, Tommy Lawrence, Terry Cooper, Gary Sprake and Mick Jones required treatment after ferocious clashes, provoking even fiercer reactions from a passionate crowd.

After the initial storm subsided, Leeds established a calm rhythm and shape that Liverpool found difficult to fathom, let alone pierce. The Reds were too keyed up to take a considered approach; cooler heads might have made them more effective, but they were all set on overpowering the champions elect. United, in contrast, kept their cool and stuck rigidly to Don Revie's blueprint.

Rob Bagchi and Paul Rogerson said in *The Unforgiven*: 'Madeley dropped deep to help out his beleaguered colleagues at every opportunity, frustrating Liverpool's forwards with a grim display of organised obduracy. Reaney and Cooper had been detailed to sit tight on Callaghan and Thompson, Liverpool's two wingers, forcing the main thrusts to go through the middle where there were massed ranks of white shirts.' Jack Charlton's aerial dominance, the assured tackling and covering of Norman Hunter and a faultless performance by Gary Sprake made the United spine a particularly tough one to best.

In front of the rearguard, United had O'Grady, Bremner, Madeley, Giles and Gray splayed across midfield to deny the Reds space.

The approach had worked hundreds of times before – Leeds were past masters at the art of blanket defence.

It was twenty-six minutes before an attempt worthy of the name. Callaghan fired wide with an ambitious 25-yard effort, but the chance marked the start of a second wind for Liverpool. They pressed hard and came close to breaking the deadlock in the thirty-fifth minute. Bobby Graham evaded United's all-consuming net to get in a cross for Alun Evans, 14 yards out. In his eagerness, the youngster snatched at the chance and fired high and wide.

There were few other chances in the first half and Leeds' confidence was boosted by achieving their first milestone of being level at half-time, but Bill Shankly got into his men's ribs during the break, urging them to raise themselves for forty-five minutes of all-out assault. The Reds had struggled to make clear opportunities, but now they managed to find some chinks in the iron curtain.

Liverpool came close to a breakthrough in the seventy-second minute. The canny Ian St John manufactured an opening with a clever lob into the penalty area that found Evans unmarked. Again, the teenager failed to provide the finish, shooting wide with the goal at his mercy.

That was as close as the Reds came and United were able to fashion some chances of their own over the last fifteen minutes. For most of the game they had left Jones an isolated figure up front, but towards the end they managed to get some reinforcements forward. On one occasion Giles nearly sent O'Grady clear, though the chance came to nothing.

There was the inevitable pounding at the United area over the frantic final minutes, but Liverpool simply did not have the wit to unlock the rearguard – the game was up and United had survived in magnificent fashion.

Billy Bremner said:

The game was one of the most thrilling that I have ever played in. We were really wound up in the right way before the game. We knew what we had to do and, mostly, that meant keeping our cool and playing our normal professional game.

The game was played at a lightning pace with Liverpool doing their best to break down our defence. However, Jack Charlton and Norman Hunter were tremendous and held it all together. In fact, Gary Sprake in goal was almost having an easy night because nothing got through the defence. We nearly sneaked one at the other end when I had a shot deflected. The minutes ticked away and when the final whistle blew I enjoyed one of the greatest experiences of my football life.

Up to that moment the Liverpool fans had been solidly behind their team, roaring them on to a possible victory. Once the final whistle went and they knew that the game and the title race was over, they put away their bias and gave us a standing ovation. We even went on a lap of honour and they cheered us as if we were their own team. It was a fantastic moment and one of the greatest gestures that I have ever experienced.

Richard Sutcliffe wrote in *Revie: Revered and Reviled*:

When referee Arthur Dimond blew the final whistle, the joy was etched across the faces of every player. Revie was similarly overjoyed but insisted on grabbing a quiet word with his inspirational captain. The United manager had told Billy Bremner before kick-off that, if they got the point they required, he must take the team to the Kop end. Bremner thought his manager was mad but Revie reinforced the point after the title had been clinched. The diminutive Scot still had his doubts but, as with everyone at Elland Road, he did what he was told by his boss and duly started to lead the Leeds team towards the famous terrace housing almost 27,000 Liverpool fans. Plus John Helm, who recalls: 'I remember seeing the Leeds lads come towards us. Billy looked reluctant, to say the least. You could hear a pin drop as they got as far as the penalty area and I did wonder how it was going to end. Eventually, this chant of "Champions, Champions, Champions…" began and, within seconds, it seemed everyone around me was joining in. The Kop could see the Liverpool players had given it everything but had lost out to the best team in the country. The reception was amazing and totally genuine. It was a magical moment, and one I will never forget.'

Anfield
Attendance: 53,750

Liverpool: Lawrence, Lawler, Strong, Smith, Yeats, Hughes, Callaghan, Graham, Evans, St John, Thompson

Leeds United: Sprake, Reaney, Cooper, Bremner, Charlton, Hunter, O'Grady, Madeley, Jones, Giles, Gray

25

Leeds United 0-1 Celtic
European Cup Semi-Final, First Leg
1 April 1970

United's European Cup semi-final against Celtic in 1970 was billed as Britain's club championship. Of course, the presence of Bremner, Lorimer and Gray in the United side, bolstered by a Welshman and an Irishman diluted Leeds' England credentials.

Celtic manager Jock Stein went to see Leeds play for the third time in twelve days when he watched them beat Manchester United in their FA Cup semi-final second replay at Bolton on 26 March. He said afterwards, 'Leeds are a fine team and played well, but I do not think they are as good as people make out down in England. There is talk about the fixture problem they face, but I don't think this is a factor... We played more games when winning the European Cup than Leeds will have done at the end of the season.'

Factually speaking, Stein might have been correct, but his words concealed the sheer intensity of United's fixture congestion. The two replays that they required to see off Manchester in the FA Cup meant that in the fifteen days from 21 March to 4 April they had to play eight times.

Asked about his team selection, Revie said gloomily, 'I hope it will be our 100 per cent team, but I don't expect them to be 100 per cent physically or mentally right after the strain we have undergone this last fortnight.' Norman Hunter was the only absentee with the knee injury that he sustained in the quarter-final against Standard Liege; Paul Madeley deputised.

Stein's selection contained seven of their European Cup-winning eleven and the manager was convinced that Jimmy Johnstone would be an ace in the hole.

Johnstone was pitched directly against United left-back Terry Cooper, widely touted at the time as one of the world's best, but Stein had no doubts, telling a friend, 'They say this Cooper is a great attacking full-back, but he's never had this tricky wee dwarf running at him for 90 minutes.'

United had yet to concede a goal in the tournament and Celtic had not scored away from home, but those records were shredded as the visitors took a lead within ninety seconds.

Auld's huge up and under from his own half came down with snow on it near the corner of United's penalty area. The normally reliable Madeley was on hand to clear but was being harried by Celtic centre forward Wallace. He allowed the ball to bounce and then misjudged its trajectory, getting under it when he tried to head away. Jack Charlton couldn't get in his attempted clearance and Wallace had the time and presence of mind to touch the ball back to Connelly, unmarked on the edge of the box. The Under-23 international's shot took a deflection off Cooper's outstretched leg, which sent it bobbling out of the reach of Gary Sprake and in at the far post.

The goal boosted Celtic's confidence and Jinky Johnstone took it on himself to give Terry Cooper the chasing of his life. Cooper, without the protective insurance of Norman Hunter, was exposed, with little cover to speak of. With Johnstone in irresistible form, Cooper had one of the worst footballing nights of his life, and no time to even think of breaking forward – at a stroke a key component of United's attacking game was neutered.

After six minutes Johnstone tricked his way past three men to make space for a shot from the edge of the area, only to be denied by Sprake.

Phil Brown: 'Celtic then gave little right winger Johnstone lashings of the ball for 20 minutes, and he was just untackleable then and after. I doubt if Elland Road has ever seen such feinting, swerving and sidestepping inside a square yard. It must have been horrible to see such an individual genius on such form in control and so fleet into the open spaces.'

He was aided and abetted in his work by Bobby Murdoch, who constantly prompted from midfield. After the schemer finished off one smart move with a fearsome shot that was touched over the bar, Lennox went narrowly wide from the corner.

Albert Barham commented in *The Guardian*:

> Don Revie had admitted that after the gruelling succession of matches his team were neither physically nor mentally fully fit for their crucial match ... It was not until the 34th minute that they were able to break the stranglehold.
>
> Giles and Bremner had worked unceasingly to get Leeds into a scoring position. They had tried to probe through the centre of the defence. They had tried to send Cooper and Reaney down the wings but all seemed to fail against the tall McNeill and Brogan, who nodded Celtic out of trouble. Then in the 34th minute, Giles lobbed a ball high into the goalmouth. Williams could not get to it, but Gemmell swept it away off the line as Jones challenged.

Seven minutes later Lorimer crossed to the near post only for Jones and Bremner to both miss from close in. Then Bremner manufactured another opening with a run down the right but when he played Lorimer in, the Scot cleared the bar from 14 yards.

United ended the half on the offensive, but it could not disguise the fact that they had been off colour and outclassed, as reported by Geoffrey Green in *The Times*:

> They looked a jaded company, full of inaccuracies in their passing, faults that could be placed even at the doorstep of the usually immaculate Bremner and Giles.
>
> Time after time, too, vast open spaces were carved in their defence such as one has not seen before all season. In attack, their one ploy seemed to be the long high cross ball aimed for the heads of Jones and Clarke. Celtic found little bother in countering that. The Scots in fact showed a far cleverer variation in their whole game; Auld drew Bremner into many a false position in midfield as he and Murdoch coolly dominated the central areas. It is not often that Bremner and Giles have to play second fiddle in this way.

Don Revie must have hoped that Leeds could revive their hopes after the break, but they were nearly the victims of another early shock. Before the first minute had elapsed,

Connelly had the ball in the net a second time. Auld fired a crossfield pass to Johnstone on the byline. He was harassed closely by Cooper, but managed to slide the ball across to Connelly, who shot home. Fortunately for Leeds, French referee Kitabdjian disallowed the goal, presumably for offside against Johnstone, though he protested long and hard. It had looked clearly as if Cooper had played him on.

If the official was lenient on United, he would even things up when his perverse decisions would rob them of European glory against Bayern in 1975.

As if acknowledging their fortune, United drew themselves together and forged some kind of grip on affairs; they created more chances in the second period, without finding the gilt-edged one that they so badly required.

They sensed that an early equaliser was essential if they were to win the game and thought they'd got it on the hour when Lorimer found Clarke in space. Unfortunately, he hesitated, perhaps looking for a better placed teammate and his uncertain effort was saved by goalkeeper Williams, who blocked with his knees. Shortly afterwards, Lorimer, Clarke and Jones all seemed to be waiting for another to seize the opportunity in front of a yawning goal when Williams punched loosely. The chance was gone before any of them could react as Gemmell hoofed clear.

On fifty-eight minutes Bremner was injured. He had fallen to the ground and struck his head in Celtic's area after a series of Leeds attacks. He struggled on gamely for ten minutes but was badly dazed. He had to go off with concussion and double vision and was replaced by Bates. It was clear he knew little of what was going on as he was helped off the pitch.

Terry Lofthouse wrote in the *Yorkshire Evening Post*:

> Bremner roamed about dazed and bewildered after being led from the contest in the 67th minute ... Les Cocker eventually managed to get him off the pitch, and for another half hour Bremner knew little about what was happening. He was ordered home and a taxi called. But suddenly he reappeared and went into the Celtic dressing rooms. Trainer Cocker and the club doctor rushed from the home dressing room and took the pale-looking Bremner back there. It was quite a while before he regained his composure.

Bremner's withdrawal saw much of the fire leave United's work, though Gray came close in the seventy-second minute. He turned past two men, hiding his intentions until the last minute, superbly concealing a fearsome right-footed drive until he struck it from the ruck. It 'made the crossbar twang like a bowstring' (Albert Barham).

Another couple of chances came but ended with anxious Leeds players ballooning them harmlessly over the crossbar as they succumbed to a 1-0 defeat.

Phil Brown summed up perfectly in the *Yorkshire Evening Post* the following day when he observed that 'the elastic had gone.'

Elland Road
Attendance: 45,505

Leeds United: Sprake, Reaney, Cooper, Bremner (Bates), Charlton, Madeley, Lorimer, Clarke, Jones, Giles, Gray

Celtic: Williams, Hay, Gemmell, Murdoch, McNeill, Brogan, Johnstone, Connelly (Hughes), Wallace, Auld, Lennox

Left: Billy Bremner in action against Wilson Piazza for Scotland in their World Cup match against Brazil on 18 June 1974. (Photo: Trinity Mirror/Mirrorpix/Alamy Stock Photo).

Below: Billy Bremner in action against Martin Peters during Scotland's home international match against England at Hampden Park. The final score was a 2-0 victory to Scotland on 18 May 1974. (Photo: Trinity Mirror/Mirrorpix/ Alamy Stock Photo).

FA Cup Quarter Final match at Elland Road. Leeds United 2-1 Tottenham Hotspur. Mike England of Spurs fighting with Billy Bremner, 18 March 1972. (Photo: Trinity Mirror/Mirrorpix/Alamy Stock Photo)

European Championship Qualifier: Scotland 1-0 Belgium. Pittodrie – Aberdeen
Scotland's Billy Bremner in action, 10 November 1971. (Photo: SNS Group/Alamy
Stock Photo)

Leeds United win the FA Cup at Wembley. Photo shows Leeds United captain, Billy Bremner, seated on the shoulders of Allan Clarke and Peter Lorimer, 6 May 1972. (Photo: Keystone Pictures USA/Alamy Stock Photo)

Billy Bremner, Leeds United captain, with manager Don Revie holding the FA Cup after their 1-0 victory over Arsenal in the FA Cup final, 6 May 1972. (Photo: Trinity Mirror/Mirrorpix/Alamy Stock Photo)

26

Leeds United 2-2 Chelsea
FA Cup Final
11 April 1970

United's failure to do themselves justice in either of their previous Wembley Cup finals had left Don Revie determined that they should put matters right in the 1970 FA Cup final. The 1965 FA Cup final and the war of League Cup attrition against Arsenal three years later were among the most dismal occasions in the history of the grand old stadium.

Leeds had enjoyed a wonderful campaign, in with a shout of the 'impossible' treble of League, Cup and European Cup until the end of March; but Everton had secured the championship and a home defeat to Celtic had left only tenuous chances in the European Cup. The Wembley showdown with old rivals Chelsea was now the only real opportunity of success.

Leeds' preparations for Wembley were less than ideal with one win in five games and Paul Reaney fracturing his leg. Paul Madeley was switched to cover for Reaney against Chelsea, allowing Norman Hunter, out since 18 March, to return alongside Jack Charlton.

The recent staging of the Horse of the Year Show had left the Wembley playing surface in horrendous condition, as recalled by Billy Bremner:

There was not a sign of the normally immaculate turf which everyone associates with Wembley. The pitch had been sanded – but you found yourself almost ankle deep in mud and sand, at times – and if Wembley's once lush turf was stamina-sapping, I can tell you that the pitch on which we played destroyed the energy of the players, as the game wore on. The pitch didn't run true – the ball came at you from awkward angles, bounced and bobbed about.

Mistakes would be inevitable on the pudding of a pitch, but United rose above the bog to give one of their best displays of the season. Their return to form owed much to the recuperation that several players had enjoyed with the title race conceded. Hunter had been the longest out of action at twenty-four days, while Cooper, Bremner, Charlton, Jones, Giles, Clarke and Sprake had enjoyed at least a week off.

Paradoxically, it was Eddie Gray, a man who had enjoyed no rest at all, who gave the most impressive performance. A week earlier against Burnley the winger had scored two brilliant goals: one a precision lob from 30 yards and the other after a master class in footwork and control that left a collection of defenders bewitched, bothered and bewildered.

Gray was to play the game of his life, weaving his light-footed magic across the gluepot of a pitch.

From the off Leeds were onto the attack, compressing play into the Chelsea half. Whenever a Blues man had the ball, United players harried him instantly, pushing for an error. Eddie McCreadie and John Dempsey were both squeezed into mistakes and it was clear this tactic would serve Leeds well.

They settled the better, with the partnership of Bremner and Giles controlling midfield, thoughtful and controlled with their distribution, piercing the areas where the Londoners were vulnerable. Lorimer and Gray were prominent on the wings with Clarke and Jones keeping Leeds defending right from the front line. It was an effective game plan.

With twenty minutes gone, Lorimer's looping centre from the left was put out for a corner by Dempsey, with Jones waiting to collect.

Charlton took up his station on Bonetti's line and rose with Clarke when Gray's corner dropped on the 6-yard line. The keeper misjudged the ball's flight as Charlton rose highest to nod down, his header trickling gently goalwards. With Harris and McCreadie on hand to clear, Chelsea skipper Harris checked, thinking his colleague had matters in hand. The ball kept low as it bounced and McCreadie swung wildly over it as it dribbled across the line. Harris and Osgood both appealed for a foul on Bonetti, who stood hands on hips in silent protest.

There was no doubt in the mind of referee Eric Jennings and he went running back to halfway.

Leeds continued to press with Gray posing Webb no end of problems. He was in complete command, the ball seemingly glued to his toes. The winger tricked, bobbed and weaved, leaving Webb on his back on several occasions.

Lorimer fed Gray on the touchline about 35 yards out – he had a clear run in on Webb, who back-pedalled away, until he felt enough was enough and jumped into the tackle. Gray checked outside him into space and readied for a cross. Webb managed to recover and lunged in for another challenge, but Gray this time smoothly danced inside. Though his shot flew well over the top, the moment epitomised the hold that Gray had established.

It looked like United would reach the break with their lead intact. They even hinted at increasing their advantage when a hopeful punt up the right channel was intercepted by Harris. He had plenty of time to find Bonetti, but the ball was weak and wide as Jones came striding across. The goalkeeper managed to clutch it on the byline, right in the corner of his area.

In the forty-first minute, Hutchinson went up with Lorimer on the edge of the Leeds box and the ball fell loose to Houseman 25 yards out. As Bremner came in to challenge, Houseman swung speculatively with his left foot.

It was by no means a fierce effort but ran low through the crowded area to Sprake's left. The keeper saw it well enough and was down in good time, but allowed it to squirm under his body and over the line for an undeserved equaliser.

The treacherous pitch clearly played a part in both first half goals, but that was little consolation to Sprake, for whom the moment was the most infamous of his career.

Leeds continued to play decent football after the break, holding the ball patiently as they waited for an opportunity to emerge.

Chelsea came close to a goal when they sustained a period of pressure in and around the Leeds area. Baldwin held the ball up well at midfield despite pressure from Giles and Clarke, before Hollins, Houseman and Osgood set up Hutchinson on the right. The Leeds defence had been sucked in and Hutchinson muscled his way outside Cooper and down the right channel towards the 6-yard box.

Sprake came out to block the first effort at the forward's feet, but the ball eventually found its way back to Hutchinson, whom Sprake then foiled twice more. Hunter cleared Osgood's follow up from underneath the bar. The ball reached the 6-yard line where Gray trapped it, moved wide and carried calmly away before being brought down by Hutchinson.

Shortly afterwards Clarke failed to control on the touchline, though he was able to rush Harris into a hasty clearance. Gray plucked it out of the air and danced toward a confrontation with Webb. He came inside and held the defender off before sliding it to Giles in the middle, some 30 yards out. The Irishman stood the ball up into the area for Lorimer to nod down across the 6-yard line. Jones hooked in an instant but weak shot, which Bonetti smothered as Bremner raced in.

A poor throw in from McCreadie allowed Leeds to recover possession and carve out another opportunity. Bremner tangled ferociously with Harris, but Clarke came away to find Lorimer. Chelsea's clearance of the Scot's cross was poor and Gray hammered a shot against the bar with Bonetti beaten.

As the game reached its eighty-third minute, it appeared that United had settled the issue when they got the second goal that they deserved. When Giles rolled the ball inside to Bremner, the Scot looked to see what was on and waited, edging his way forward. Giles had continued his run to the byline and finally Bremner chipped an inch perfect ball inside the full-back to the Irishman. His cross fell invitingly for Clarke to twist like a snake into a diving header before Harris could react. It was a wonderful effort, beating Bonetti all ends up, but struck the foot of the post and ran out to the right. Jones was in the right spot to fire it back across the keeper and into the net off the back post.

The entire Leeds party went wild, convinced that Chelsea would never fight back from such a late blow.

They were wrong. With four minutes remaining, Chelsea won a free-kick on the left when Charlton tangled with Osgood. The ball ran back to Sprake and he tried to punt it into the crowd to waste time. But he sliced it and it went straight to Harris who took the free-kick quickly, slipping it inside to Hollins. His clipped cross to the front post was met perfectly by Hutchinson diving to nod home.

United were in despair.

There was time for another close shave at the other end. When Jones was crowded out in the Chelsea area, the ball came out to Gray and he curled a cross to the back of the area. Lorimer nodded it down and Clarke adjusted his feet perfectly to whip into a wonderful volley that crashed against Bonetti's bar and away.

The cloying pitch had sapped the energy of the players and the extra thirty minutes rarely promised a breakthrough. In the fifth minute, Gray set up Giles, but the Irishman's volley was scrambled off the line by Webb. In the closing seconds Sprake pulled off a reflex save from a goalbound shot by Houseman. But that was it.

The game over, the players went out together on a joint lap of honour after the first drawn final since 1912.

It had been the most magnificent of finals, quite the most exciting for years, and, as Revie mused, 'just think what sort of game it would have been on a pitch!'

Wembley Stadium
Attendance: 100,000

Leeds United: Sprake, Madeley, Cooper, Bremner, Charlton, Hunter, Lorimer, Clarke, Jones, Giles, Gray

Chelsea: Bonetti, Webb, McCreadie, Hollins, Dempsey, Harris (Hinton), Baldwin, Houseman, Osgood, Hutchinson, Cooke

27

Celtic 2-1 Leeds United
European Cup Semi-Final, Second Leg
15 April 1970

Burdened by a 1-0 defeat from the first game, Leeds United were underdogs when they travelled to Scotland to meet Celtic in the second leg of their European Cup semi-final.

Both teams came into the game fresh from domestic Cup finals. Celtic had been the victims of what the *Daily Record* dubbed 'the biggest upset in a final since the war,' Aberdeen thumping them 3-1, while Leeds had drawn 2-2 with Chelsea.

When the game kicked off, Leeds enjoyed the first sortie into enemy territory with Jack Charlton thumping the ball long for Eddie Gray and Mick Jones to combine to provide possession for Billy Bremner. The Scot attempted to get his men going with a searching through ball towards Celtic's area, but it was swallowed up by the home defence and then the Scots took over.

Celtic forced five corners in the opening eight minutes and it was their midfield combination that provided the platform. Jimmy Johnstone continued where he had left off at Elland Road, only now he could enjoy the constant support of young Davie Hay from right-back. Norman Hunter provided some reassurance to Terry Cooper but it made little difference; Johnstone was even more of a menace than he had been in the first leg.

The torture started early on as Johnstone combined smartly with Hay down the right to win a free-kick out of a desperately lunging Cooper. Murdoch played the ball short to Johnstone but it came back to him as the winger was tackled. Murdoch hammered a long-range drive that struck Gary Sprake's left hand post and was cleared by Charlton. The centre half angrily berated his keeper, who looked to have knocked his head.

Paul Madeley raced through the centre, beating two home defenders as he edged to the left and found Peter Lorimer on the wing. He cut the ball back to Bremner, who fed it on with a swinging pass to Gray on the right wing, but as he attempted to trick his marker, the ball ran out for a throw in to Celtic.

That preceded an unexpected breakthrough by United. With fourteen minutes gone, some anxious Celtic defending allowed Hunter to pick up the ball 40 yards out. He fed Bremner who set off on a run, steadying himself about 25 yards out for a strike. It was as if all the tensions, cares and woes of the previous month were erased in one fell swoop as the United captain exploded into action.

Bremner launched himself into possibly the finest shot of his life. The little Scot had scored many vital goals for United, but it's doubtful whether he ever pulled off a cleaner strike, finishing with both feet in the air as the ball arrowed towards its target, cannoning into the net after crashing against the junction between post and bar. Goalkeeper Evan Williams could only stand transfixed.

The crowd fell remarkably silent for a moment that seemed like an hour, and there was suddenly a spring in the Leeds step with Bremner competing manfully in the middle of the field.

For a while the issue teetered in the balance with first Leeds and then Celtic having a decent moment. United had gained their share of midfield and looked to spring forward with quick through balls, mainly emanating from Bremner, but Celtic enjoyed the bulk of the play and offered the greater threat through their readiness to commit men into attack.

They cranked up the pressure on Sprake's goal. Hughes was having a fine game and a long ball forward gave him space but his shot from 18 yards was gathered confidently by the keeper.

Johnstone created more panic with a series of twists and turns before slipping the ball to the overlapping Hay, who sent in a fierce shot. Celtic's appeal for hands was echoed thunderously by the partisan home crowd but the referee waved away the claims.

After thirty-five minutes, Connelly turned into space before chipping forward for Lennox to dart through the middle and flick the ball past the onrushing Sprake at the penalty spot. It looked all ends up a goal but Madeley recovered to hook off the line.

It was all Celtic now with the ball coming back repeatedly at the United defence. Johnstone was a livewire and constantly probed for an opening.

The greatest threat came from that flank and when Johnstone was freed after thirty-nine minutes by a long ball, he tricked Cooper but was blatantly hacked down by Bremner. From the resultant free-kick, Auld's cross reached Gemmell at the back post. He fired it back across the goal line, but Cooper blocked it out and Sprake dived onto the loose ball.

Clarke was booked for a nasty follow through on Hay, but the defender was quickly up and on with the game. His attitude was typical of the home men, who were taking some rough treatment in great spirit. Auld could be as nasty as any of the men in United's ranks, and after forty-two minutes Jones was carried off with a deep gash on his right shin. For a time, there were fears he would not return. Bremner: 'It was a terrible, terrible tackle … His leg was in a terrible state at half-time. Well, I chased Bertie a few times that night. He knew I was after him. But no chance. He was too fly.'

As the first period drew to a close, Bremner was happy to concede the corner when Hughes broke down the left. Auld flashed it to the near post but it was blocked by a combination of Sprake and Hunter. The two men crashed into each other in the process and required attention. There was no time to take the second flag kick with the referee signalling for half-time.

Jones was restored to action at the start of the second half, but the next ten minutes were nightmarish for him and his colleagues.

After forty-seven minutes Johnstone fed Auld down the right and the ball was fired on for Hay to chase Hunter all the way down to the byline. The defender had little choice but to concede the corner. The ball was played short to Auld and his drilled waist-high cross was met in the middle by Hughes diving ahead of Charlton to nod home inside the far post and bring Celtic level on the night.

Only minutes later Auld played a ball inside the right-back for Hughes to chase down hard. Hunter was neck and neck with him but checked as he saw Sprake coming out to collect as the ball reached the line. Hughes refused to give way and crashed recklessly into the keeper as he dived bravely to gather. It was a terrible collision but Hughes displayed little sympathy, glancing back just once as Sprake received treatment.

The keeper was stretchered off the pitch with David Harvey replacing him. Within a couple of minutes, he was under pressure, the ball reaching Johnstone in acres of space down the right flank. The winger laid it square for Murdoch, coming up at pace, to send a low shot under Harvey's dive and into the net to give Celtic a 3-1 aggregate lead.

That was in the fifty-third minute and in those first eight minutes of the second period, United's Euro hopes had evaporated. Celtic could take their foot off the accelerator with Leeds forced to dispense with any thoughts of containment.

That combination made for an interesting final thirty minutes with Charlton throwing caution to the wind and storming upfield at every opportunity.

Clarke got on the end of a long punt forward to beat his man in the area and nod the ball down for Giles on the 6-yard line, but the whistle had already gone for a foul against the Leeds striker.

Leeds brought Bates on for Lorimer after seventy-one minutes and thrust Bremner up front as a supplementary striker.

As the game entered its final sixty seconds, Bremner fastened on to a neat pass by Gray on the edge of the Celtic box and turned and shot, but Williams collected the ball. His hoofed clearance reached Hughes on the left. He left Hunter in his wake at the touchline, cut inside and rounded Harvey only to see Madeley block his goal bound effort.

That was the last action of an enthralling evening's football. The combatants exchanged jerseys and Celtic took off on a celebratory lap of honour as the United players trooped off disconsolately to the dressing room, their European Cup challenge in tatters.

Hampden Park
Attendance: 136,505

Celtic: Williams, Hay, Gemmell, Murdoch, McNeill, Brogan, Johnstone, Connelly, Hughes, Auld, Lennox

Leeds: Sprake (Harvey), Madeley, Cooper, Bremner, Charlton, Hunter, Lorimer (Bates), Clarke, Jones, Giles, Gray

28

Leeds United 1-2 Chelsea
FA Cup Final Replay
29 April 1970

If the drawn FA Cup final between Chelsea and Leeds demonstrated much that was good about English football, the replay won a reputation for being the dirtiest final ever.

Three decades later, former referee David Elleray reviewed a DVD of the match against the standards set by modern-day refereeing. He concluded that Leeds should have had seven bookings and three dismissals (Giles, Bremner and Charlton), while Chelsea deserved thirteen bookings, including three each for Webb, Harris and Cooke.

Eric Jennings, the referee in charge of the actual game, took a *laissez-faire* approach, offering plenty of leeway and booking just one player, the Londoners' Ian Hutchinson.

Chelsea set their stall out to prevent Leeds from repeating their Wembley dominance. Eddie Gray had given David Webb a roasting and now manager Dave Sexton switched Webb and Ron Harris, lining the famous Chelsea hard man up against Gray with the intention of kicking him out of the game. Webb's reckless challenges were more easily compensated for in the centre of defence, where his colleagues could protect him.

With a television audience estimated at 32 million watching the game, Leeds were instantly onto the attack – within the first minute Lorimer's cross hit Dempsey and the deflection almost took it into the Chelsea net. Then Gray rounded Harris down the left touchline; he managed to get in a low cross before the tackle came in. Mick Jones flicked the ball on with Webb unable to get to him and Bonetti got down well to touch the effort wide.

After twelve minutes Chelsea had another escape. Cooper's long centre swung away from Bonetti and Lorimer turned it back across goal. Gray could have shot but returned it to Lorimer. He went for the spectacular and only succeeded in sending the ball wide.

United continued to press and they ratcheted up the pace, forcing Chelsea back onto defence. There was an exchange of punches between Hunter and McCreadie as tempers frayed and with the crowd's attention diverted, Gray took the opportunity to run into space, his shot running narrowly wide.

In the twenty-fifth minute, Dempsey attempted a back-pass to Bonetti with the keeper miles away from his station. Lorimer beat him to the ball, only to see his shot from an acute angle saved on the line by McCreadie.

On the half hour, Bonetti was injured in an aerial clash with Jones as the two went for a steepling Madeley centre. There was a mass protest from Chelsea at what they saw as flagrant foul play. Action was held up for three minutes while the keeper received treatment and he was badly limping when play restarted.

Chelsea responded by launching an all-out assault on the United goal. It cost them heavily, for in the thirty-sixth minute Leeds took a deserved lead after coolly playing themselves out of trouble.

Gray brought play away from the Leeds box via a cool one-two with Giles before feeding on to Clarke, 10 yards inside his own half. He set off on a wonderful run, escaping three heavy challenges from different Blues men. Each time it looked like he would be clattered but a combination of pace and deft feints took Clarke through the eye of a needle and left defenders sprawling.

He slipped the ball short to Jones and let his partner carry the move on. The centre forward set off on a storming run, coming away from Hollins and Harris and resisting intense pressure from McCreadie to make his way into the Chelsea area. From there he hammered a thunderous right-footed shot across Bonetti and into the net.

Leeds still held that lead at the break.

Almost immediately after the resumption Cooke and Clarke started kicking seven bells out of each other. Referee Jennings turned a blind eye, as he had throughout the first half, but finally, there came an incident which he could not ignore. Charlton and Osgood were involved in a scramble near the touchline and the striker took Charlton out. The big man completely lost it, got to his feet, stormed after Osgood and scythed him mercilessly to the ground. Even then Jennings merely gave them a severe talking to and no names were taken. It was the sixthy-fifth minute before the referee's tolerance was finally tested too far. Osgood and Bremner tangled and when the Scot appeared to be hacking at the fallen Chelsea man, the referee thought it worth only another cool glance. Hutchinson rushed up impetuously to push Bremner to the ground and was cautioned. It was the only booking of the night.

Leeds still drove forward, pressing to increase their lead. Hunter won a ball 25 yards from the Blues' goal line and slipped it to Gray on the left. He flicked it back to Cooper, who played the ball forward and twisted and turned around two defenders to catch it and loft over a cross. Jones challenged in the air and the ball ran out to the edge of the area for the onrushing Giles to strike low for the bottom corner. It was deflected by a Chelsea man and scraped the post and the side netting, with Bonetti stranded.

Geoffrey Green noted a change in the tide:

> Where once the great steam roller of Leeds had driven forward, with Giles and Bremner putting Jones, Gray and Lorimer into full stride, and with Clarke adding some highly cultured and sensitive touches, it had all been one way. Now it was the elegant Osgood, the elusive Cooke and the non-stop Hollins who oiled Chelsea's wheels at last.
>
> With ten minutes left they suddenly were level. Theirs, too, was a beautiful goal: more complicated, more finely ingrained, more liquid and created virtually out of nothing. Here was the poetry of football and it came with a magical exchange of passes between Hollins, Hutchinson, Osgood and then the hard-running Cooke. Over came Cooke's perfect chip and there was Osgood infiltrating from the left to the blind side to head a magnificent goal.

United's defence had been guilty of a desperate lack of concentration; Osgood found a huge gap with five United defenders querying pathetically who was picking the striker up. For a team with such a mean defensive reputation, it was an astonishing lapse.

In the normal time that remained there was some fierce and frenetic action. Bremner was heavily involved: United had justifiable claims for a penalty ignored when McCreadie appeared to be intent on decapitating his Scottish international colleague.

When Cooper's high centre bounced out from an aerial challenge, McCreadie leapt up feet first into a wild and dangerous high kick that took Bremner in the forehead. The Scot was left writhing on the ground holding his head for what seemed an age.

Referee Jennings saw Cooper pick up the ball and shape for a shot. He played advantage but none was taken as Chelsea blocked the chance. Osgood and Hutchinson went away to fashion an opportunity which ran narrowly wide of Harvey's post. Bremner required lengthy treatment before he was fit to carry on.

Following that he tangled heavily with Hutchinson and received a rebuke from Jennings; and finally, he was sent crashing to the ground as he raced in on goal, reacting angrily when more penalty claims were refused.

Two hundred and ten minutes of football failed to fashion a conclusion and the two teams had to line up for another half hour of hard labour.

Don Revie sought valiantly to rally his men to one last effort, imploring them for one final push. He got a response, despite the tired limbs and minds, but it was the Londoners who got their noses in front.

One minute before the end of the first period of extra time, Chelsea broke the deadlock, taking the lead for the first time.

The goal came courtesy of one of Hutchinson's trademark long throws. Charlton met the ball at the front post but could only succeed in flicking the ball in a lofty and inviting arc across goal. Harvey had tried to come through and punch clear but couldn't find an avenue past Charlton. In the melee that followed Webb rose above Gray and Cooper at the back post to bundle the ball home.

That reverse should have been enough to kill off any fight that remained in the exhausted Leeds men, but they forced themselves into a final despairing assault, throwing everything into headlong attack. It was a wild-eyed attempt to claw something from an amazing season that, when once so much glory had beckoned, now promised to leave them empty handed.

Osgood was replaced with eight minutes to go by Hinton as the Londoners manned the barricades, but he set up an opportunity for Hutchinson before he departed, with Harvey left unprotected as his team chased a late equaliser. Hutchinson put the chance away but the goal was disallowed for offside.

That was a rare excursion upfield for Chelsea as virtually the entire fifteen minutes were played out in and around the Londoners' area.

Leeds could not turn their domination into a goal and were left distraught at the end. Billy Bremner commented:

As you can imagine our dressing room was the most miserable place on earth after the game. Nobody wanted to look at their medals. It was the boss who brought us back to life again. He didn't say much but his well-chosen words gave us something to think about. He simply said: 'We've got to start all over again. We've done it before and we can do it again.' Somehow that changed our focus from what had just happened to what we were going to make happen in the future.

It was the most galling and inequitable of setbacks for a club that had become hardened by a succession of near misses over the previous six years.

Geoffrey Green in *The Times*: 'Leeds, like Sisyphus, have pushed three boulders almost to the top of three mountains and are now left to see them all back in the dark of the valley.'

Old Trafford
Attendance: 62,078

Leeds United: Harvey, Madeley, Cooper, Bremner, Charlton, Hunter, Lorimer, Clarke, Jones, Giles, Gray

Chelsea: Bonetti, Harris, McCreadie, Hollins, Dempsey, Webb, Baldwin, Cooke, Osgood (Hinton), Hutchinson, Houseman

29

Liverpool 0-1 Leeds United
European Fairs Cup Semi-Final, First Leg
14 April 1971

A long and healthy tradition of respect and rivalry links Liverpool and Leeds United, dating back to the days when Bill Shankly and Don Revie led the two clubs from the wilderness of Second Division football to the top of the European game.

After United secured the League title with a goalless draw at Anfield in April 1969, Shankly began to rebuild, blooding a host of youngsters, many of them snapped up from the lower divisions: the team was transformed as Ray Clemence, Larry Lloyd, Emlyn Hughes, Steve Heighway and John Toshack replaced regulars like Tommy Lawrence, Ron Yeats, Roger Hunt and Ian St John.

By contrast, of the Leeds team that played in the 1965 Cup final, Sprake, Reaney, Bremner, Charlton, Hunter and Giles were still regular first teamers in 1971.

The two northern giants met in the Fairs Cup semi-finals, guaranteeing England at least one berth in the final of the competition.

Peter Lorimer was injured, but Revie had the significant consolation of being able to recall Billy Bremner for his first appearance since 23 February. For the Scot, the season had been one long injury nightmare.

Bremner had managed only twenty-five minutes of first team football in three months. He had struggled through the autumn with damaged knee ligaments, then suffered an ankle injury against Rotherham in early January before sustaining a hairline fracture in his left leg when making his comeback.

It was clearly a gamble to recall the skipper, but Revie would always select a barely fit Bremner ahead of other players who were 100 per cent; the captain was a totem with a track record of snatching decisive goals in big games.

United were favourites, despite going into the game on a run of one victory in five games and the Reds being undefeated at home all season. Paul Madeley's goal in the 1-1 draw in December 1970 was the first scored by a United player at Anfield in five years.

Bremner's first act of the night turned out well: he won the toss and decided to defend the Kop end in the first half, a tactical gamble designed to undermine any second half surge from the Reds.

Understandably, Bremner took a while to get going but after he had found the pace of the game, his was a significant contribution.

Despite Liverpool's early dominance, it was seventeen minutes before they created an opening, Evans failing to get his head to a Callaghan centre.

United responded instantly, with Clarke putting the ball past Clemence, though the effort was chalked off for offside.

Goalkeeper Sprake injured his back early on but defied his pain to show great form, making fine saves from Lawler, Lindsay and Heighway.

Leeds rose to the challenge and were unlucky not to take the lead after twenty-five minutes. Bremner got possession and fed Madeley, whose shot was well saved by Clemence.

It was nip and tuck from then on, with United playing mostly on the break, but they looked solid and steady at the back. At the interval, there was no goal and little sign of one.

Shankly gave his players a flea in the ear during the break and they went at Leeds with renewed vigour. Evans fluffed the chance of the night, finding only the upright when Toshack's quick centre left him unmarked 5 yards from goal.

Leeds were more calculating with their openings and opened the scoring after sixty-seven minutes. Bremner, who had played in an advanced role throughout, drew a foul wide on the right and was waiting when Giles fired the free-kick into the area. It bypassed all the Liverpool men and sailed invitingly toward the Scot, who jackknifed to nod home.

Bremner's joyous colleagues raced to congratulate their restored leader. Barry Foster in the *Yorkshire Post*: 'The feelings of the whole Leeds side were epitomised by Charlton who ran thirty yards with his hands waving joyfully in the air to pick up and congratulate his captain.'

It was the 100th goal scored by Leeds in the campaign and, fittingly enough, it came in United's 50th Fairs Cup-tie; the landmark had been reached in just five seasons' worth of competition.

The goal was the signal for Liverpool to throw themselves into all-out attack. They brought on Graham and Thompson and penned United back in their area. Sprake preserved the lead with a wonderful save after seventy minutes from Toshack. Then Hunter cleared a Lloyd shot off his goal line.

Heighway put Hughes through but he got the ball tangled up between his feet and Sprake combined with Charlton to snuff out the danger.

The gamble of recalling Bremner paid handsome dividends and despite lacking in match fitness, his presence was enough to inspire his colleagues to one of their classic away performances. Though he took some time to get going, in the end it was as if he had never been away.

Don Warters said in the *Yorkshire Evening Post*:

The message at Anfield was simple and shattering. Billy Bremner, Leeds United's dynamic leader, is back in business … With less than half an hour's first team football behind him in the past three months, Bremner led his team magnificently to a satisfying 1-0 victory over Liverpool.

His golden goal doesn't put United through the semi-final but it takes them a big step along the way to a third appearance in the Fairs Cup final for they have a real advantage for the second leg at Elland Road on April 28.

Bremner has had better games, but considering he played in a friendly match only 24 hours earlier he made a famous comeback.

It took him 20 minutes to become accustomed to the pace of the match but then he came more and more into affairs and played a vital forward role which culminated in him heading the goal in the 67th minute following Giles' well-flighted free-kick from the left.

A good goal it was, good enough to momentarily silence the mighty Kop.

Leeds have managed quite well without Bremner over the past months but there is no doubt that the Scot's presence is a psychological boost for the side.

Anfield
Attendance: 52,877

Liverpool: Clemence, Lawler, Lindsay, Smith, Lloyd, Hughes, Callaghan (Graham), Evans (Thompson), Heighway, Toshack, Hall

Leeds United: Sprake, Reaney (Davey), Cooper, Bremner, Charlton, Hunter, Bates, Clarke, Jones, Giles, Madeley

30

Leeds United 1-1 West Bromwich Albion
First Division
17 April 1971

The history of Leeds United is littered with controversy involving officials, and possibly the stormiest aftermath of all was provoked by a uniquely personal interpretation of the offside law, which led to the name of a new pantomime villain being inscribed indelibly in the Leeds United Book of Injustices.

When an out-of-sorts West Bromwich Albion visited Elland Road for a First Division clash in April 1971, the result seemed a foregone conclusion: Albion had lost every one of their six League games at Elland Road since United's return to the First Division in 1964; they had not won away from the Hawthorns since December 1969; indeed, it had been six weeks since they had last enjoyed a victory anywhere and they had gained just three points from their previous seven games.

Though Leeds' momentum had been stayed by a 3-1 defeat at Chelsea at the end of March, they remained two points clear of Arsenal at the top of the table. The Gunners had two games in hand and had won seven straight games in the League so were breathing hard on the pacemakers' necks.

Don Revie recalled Eddie Gray after an absence of eighteen weeks, while Billy Bremner was making his first League appearance since February.

The first quarter of an hour of the game was played out exclusively in the Albion half as United sought desperately for an early goal. But the Albion players were in determined mood and worked like Trojans to deny their hosts any clear-cut opportunities.

Whenever a Leeds player had possession, he was quickly pressed. An early ball from Gray found Mick Jones on the right, but Albion centre half John Wile was touch tight to his back, shepherding him away from the goal where he could do no damage.

When Mick Bates found Gray 20 yards out, his drive had insufficient force behind it and goalkeeper Jim Cumbes gathered it comfortably, offering no prospect of a loose ball to the onrushing Allan Clarke.

Albion's attempts at easing the pressure were predicated on the long ball, though this provided easy fare for Norman Hunter and Terry Cooper, allowing them to give Johnny Giles the possession he required to direct operations. The Irishman contrived one move that allowed the overlapping Cooper to lob a centre to Clarke on the edge of the area. The England striker could get no power in a header which rolled tamely to Cumbes.

Leeds were betraying their anxiety as the midlanders carved out some openings of their own and after nineteen minutes it was Albion who broke the deadlock. As the Baggies came out to challenge the advancing United defence, Jack Charlton tried a square pass on the halfway line, but it found only Jeff Astle, who arced it through the inside right channel for Colin Suggett. He made ground and speared a low ball to Tony Brown, racing through a square defence to the edge of the area. Brown accepted the opportunity coolly and slid the ball first time low into the corner.

The goal prompted an instant response from United. Charlton came up for a corner and was still there, waiting for Giles' high ball back in after Albion partially cleared the first cross. Leeds were awarded an indirect free-kick on the penalty spot when Charlton was obstructed as he tried to meet the ball. Play was held up for a minute and a half as referee Ray Tinkler strove schoolmasterly to press a ten-man wall back the required distance. His efforts were almost comic in their lameness. The Albion line was no more than 5 yards away when, at the third time of asking, Gray fired it goalwards, only to see his shot smothered by the defensive barrier.

The United players protested vehemently at every questionable challenge. Their usual assurance was missing, they rushed their moves, and too many passes were wild and hurried. In their haste, they failed to build any cohesive pattern.

Don Revie brought Nigel Davey on for Bates at half-time with the intention of releasing Cooper into a permanent offensive role. The change brought early promise and Gray soon had an opportunity, but flashed it over the top of Cumbes' goal.

Albion still offered a goal threat and when Suggett outpaced Hunter to a through ball, he found Brown on the edge of the box. The Albion man saw his first shot blocked by Sprake's feet and then he could only put his follow up into Sprake's hands on the 6-yard line.

Hunter worked his way with some neat footwork through the inside left channel to find Cooper. The full-back's cross brought fervent cries for hands as it struck an Albion defender but the referee would have none of it.

United took the opportunity to break out and when Bremner sought to get away into space at halfway, there was an ugly-looking tangle with Lovett. It looked like the Scot had lost it as he lashed out with his elbow in the direction of his tormenter's face, but in the end nothing came of the clash.

United used the free-kick well and carved out a genuine threat as Cooper fired in a telling cross. It ran out to the far side and Gray's instant centre was nodded into the net by Jones, but the referee blew for offside, sparking some angry mutterings from the crowd.

Bremner was again baulked unfairly as he made space with some decent footwork around 30 yards from the goal, though he managed to find Davey to his left. The substitute's lofted cross allowed Clarke to get a headed flick that looped agonisingly towards Cumbes' left-hand post before the keeper dived to tip it round for a corner.

Gray's inswinging flag kick was cleared, but Giles fired in a snap volley to the falling ball. Again, Cumbes was the master.

Leeds again appealed in vain for a penalty when Wile hacked down Clarke as he chased a long ball forward into the area but Albion were disallowed a goal for offside when Suggett followed in on Hope's long range effort as it came back off the diving Sprake.

That was the prelude for disaster, as United forsook all pretence of defence. When Hunter brought United forward in the sixty-ninth minute, his misplaced crossfield pass was intercepted by Brown who raced forward. The linesman's flag was instantly raised as Suggett, yards offside and the only man in the United half apart from Sprake, ran forward into the empty space. Brown hesitated, seemingly knowing the game was up as the hapless defenders hesitated.

But Ray Tinkler waved away the flag, insisting that there was no offence. Brown picked his way on towards the unguarded area and the oncoming Sprake. As the goalkeeper advanced, Brown slipped the ball forward to Astle, also looking suspiciously offside. The centre forward obliged with a simple tap in.

The ground was a sea of chaos as it became clear that Tinkler was going to allow the goal to stand. The United players and Don Revie were frantic with anger, ushering the linesman over to intervene with the referee. Tinkler consulted with his assistant, but would only confirm his original conclusion – the goal was good!

Bremner was beside himself with fury, angrily berating the referee and looking as if he would do him genuine harm. His indignation was echoed around the stadium, triggering scenes the like of which Elland Road had never seen. There was an invasion of supporters. The police response was immediate and effective, blocking all attempts at interference, but four minutes passed before order was restored.

When play restarted, there was not even a semblance of calm. United simply flew into the attack. Making headway was hard but with two minutes remaining, Clarke raced onto a ball into the area and flicked it smartly through the gap between Cumbes and his right-hand upright. It was a piece of classic finishing by Clarke and gave United the faint whiff of a revival.

Injury time seemed to go on forever with almost every player packed into the third of the pitch nearest to Cumbes' goal. The United assaults were frenetic, but there was never a genuine chance of an equaliser.

Finally, Tinkler blew the whistle and put United out of their misery, their championship hopes scattered to the four winds.

The result effectively cost United the title; the pitch invasion led to Elland Road being closed for the start of the following season, a decision which crippled that championship challenge. It was a desperate afternoon.

Elland Road
Attendance: 36,812

Leeds United: Sprake, Reaney, Cooper, Bremner, Charlton, Hunter, Bates (Davey), Clarke, Jones, Giles, Gray

West Bromwich: Cumbes, Hughes, Merrick, Lovett, Wile, Kaye, Suggett, Brown, Astle, Hope, Hartford

31

Juventus 2-2 Leeds United
European Fairs Cup Final, First Leg
28 May 1971

It had been another season of 'if onlys' for United. Having led the First Division table for virtually the entire year, they were undone by the remorseless, nagging pursuit of Arsenal. The Gunners' habit of grinding out win after win eventually wore down Leeds, who ended runners-up for the fourth time in seven years.

As the dust settled on a disappointing and injury-strewn campaign, there was one final opportunity for the Elland Road club to secure some silverware.

A magnificent victory at Liverpool in the first leg of the Fairs Cup semi-final provided the foundation for a place in United's third Fairs final in five attempts and they duly completed the job with a goalless draw at Elland Road.

Leeds' opponents in the final were Juventus, re-emerging as one of the giants of Italian football. Former Inter captain Armando Picchi, who led that club to three Scudetti and a couple of European Cups in the sixties, inspired a Juve revival after his appointment as coach in 1970.

The Italian club was in sombre mood as the final neared: thirty-five-year-old Picchi was in the final stages of a battle against cancer and was to lose that struggle the day after the first leg. The Czech coach of Juve's youth team, Cestmír Vycpálek, took control for the final.

The heavy downpour that had commenced in the afternoon was still in full sway, making the contest a lottery. The hosts had most of the possession and forced two corners in the first three minutes.

Lorimer responded for Leeds by letting fly from 35 yards; it was obvious that even the most speculative efforts had a chance with the conditions making it a nightmare for keepers. Clean handling was a distinct challenge, but Gary Sprake quietened growing mutterings regarding his form with a succession of fine saves, first at Capello's feet and then fielding safely after diving to Causio's deflected effort.

After twenty minutes, it became clear that Eddie Gray could not continue. The shoulder injury that kept him out of the previous week's Scotland international had been aggravated and he left the field with his arm in a sling.

Juventus knew attack was obligatory and they continued to do much of the pressing. From one of their assaults, they nearly opened the scoring after twenty-two minutes, when Anastasi's shot struck Madeley and was nearly deflected into the net. Sprake parried it and when Anastasi got to the loose ball he could only crash it against a post.

Back came Leeds for Giles to manufacture enough room to fire in an effort from 30 yards. The crossbar denied what would have been a tremendous goal in the final dangerous movement of the first period.

The players came out for the second half in fresh new strips, ready to resume battle, but it was clear that playing on would lead to farcical scenes. Within six minutes Dutch referee Laurens van Ravens held an impromptu conference with his linesman and declared the match abandoned, to the relief of most reasonable people.

It was clearly the correct decision, and Juve danced with glee, but Billy Bremner protested angrily. United were halfway to the draw that they sought and understandably disappointed at having to start again.

There was another thunderstorm on the Thursday afternoon, but Friday was blessed with bright sunshine and the restaged game kicked off as planned that evening.

Juventus were straight into their stride though the pace was more sedate than in the first game, allowing Leeds to settle.

Don Revie had promised that his team would go for goals, though most people expected a defensive approach, with Madeley there to provide his customary insurance in front of the rearguard. However, the utility man was surprisingly ready to reinforce his forwards.

United paid a heavy price for their sense of adventure. With twenty-seven minutes gone, Juventus opened the scoring. Cooper was off on a penetrative left wing dribble when Haller dispossessed him at halfway. The German found Anastasi, who in turn flicked to Causio, who fired the ball goalwards. Bettega got on the blind side of Reaney to fire past Sprake.

Five minutes later, to the derision of the home supporters, Clarke was booked after kicking Morini. It looked like retaliation against some hard buffeting by the Italian international.

Juve came close to taking a 2-0 lead when Anastasi and Charlton raced side by side after a forward pass. The Italian outpaced the defender and Charlton lunged into a desperate challenge, which Anastasi did well to ride. However, he rushed his shot and it flew wide.

That was the final opportunity of the half and Leeds went in at the break disappointed to be behind. They had shown enough to offer hope that they could take something from the game, and within three minutes of the restart they were back on terms.

When Lorimer fed Madeley 25 yards out, it would have been all too predictable for Madeley, to maintain possession, but instead he chanced his arm, letting fly at goal. It wasn't the most powerful of shots but took a deflection off Salvadore before beating Piloni to bring United level.

The goal heartened Leeds but they could not maintain their equality for long. After fifty-five minutes the Italians took a 2-1 lead when Capello fired a wonderful drive from the edge of the box into the top corner. That was the signal for Juve to show some of their best short passing moves as they took control.

If Juventus expected Leeds to fade, they were sadly mistaken as the Yorkshiremen rallied bravely, 'like a relentless tide,' according to Geoffrey Green in *The Times*.

Shortly before the goal, Anastasi had made a glaring miss, ballooning the ball over the bar from 10 yards. The striker had wasted several opportunities and was getting the bird from the home supporters before he was replaced by Novellini in the seventy-second minute. At the same time Revie took the opportunity to bring on Bates for Jones, allowing Bremner to push forward into attack. For once, though, it was not the Scot who got the goal, but the substitute.

With Juventus appealing in vain for a penalty, Leeds took the opportunity for a swift counter attack. Giles centred from the left and the cross was pushed away rather than being collected by the outrushing Piloni. Bates came out of nowhere to connect beautifully and hammer it home. It was only Bates' second touch of the game and Furino could only help the ball on into the roof of the net.

Minutes later, things might have got even better for Leeds. There were concerted appeals from the entire United party when Spinosi prevented Bremner reaching a dangerous ball in the Juventus penalty area by palming the ball away. It looked an obvious penalty but the appeals were ignored by the referee.

There were no further goals and at the end Leeds were more than satisfied with the 2-2 scoreline. With away goals counting double in the event of a draw, they had put themselves in pole position.

As on so many other major occasions, Billy Bremner had led his men from the front and provided a rallying point, as reported by Paul Wilcox in *The Guardian*: 'Leeds had a magnificent commander in Bremner, who urged his colleagues to shrug off the cares of being in arrears, and engineered Leeds' survival by his command in midfield.'

Stadio Communale, Turin
Attendance: 45,000

Juventus: Piloni; Spinosi, Salvadore, Marchetti, Furino, Morini, Haller, Capello, Causio, Anastasi (Novellini), Bettega

Leeds United: Sprake; Reaney, Cooper, Bremner, Charlton, Hunter, Lorimer, Clarke, Jones (Bates), Giles, Madeley

32

Leeds United 1-1 Juventus
European Fairs Cup Final, Second Leg
2 June 1971

By the beginning of June 1971, most British footballers had their feet up somewhere in the sun; for the players of Leeds United there was no such tranquillity. On the second day of the month they faced Juventus in the second leg of the Fairs Cup final.

The first meeting had finished 2-2; should the return also end with honours even, United's away goals would be gold in the bank.

The United team that took the Elland Road pitch boasted a sharp new look; a scripted LUFC symbol had replaced the customary owl badge on their shirts, with uniformly short sleeves mitigating the summer temperatures.

Juventus won the toss and Gary Sprake had to shield his eyes from fierce evening sunlight. The wind was also in the Italians' favour at the start, but it was Leeds who made the early running, knowing that an early goal would consolidate their advantage.

As in the first leg, United made extensive use of the high cross, calculating that the Italians would struggle to cope with their aerial ability.

Terry Cooper was soon onto the offensive with the first of a host of sparkling runs down the flank. The left-back was prominent throughout the contest.

With twelve minutes gone, the referee awarded United a free-kick out on the left and Jack Charlton went forward to take his customary station. When the defender rose with his markers to challenge for Billy Bremner's floated ball, it dropped loose. Clarke was on it in a split second, swivelling to turn and fire first time into the bottom left-hand corner.

Leeds then twice went close in a matter of minutes to increasing their lead. Clarke's curled effort and Madeley's drive each threatened a goal, but Juve proved they were no easy touch by drawing level in the twentieth minute.

Causio intercepted Madeley's crossfield pass to Cooper and sprang off swift interplay with Furino that brought them within touching distance of the United box. Anastasi ghosted away from his marker to glide free on the right and take the ball, sliding it past Sprake.

United shaded the first half, although Anastasi came close to giving Juve the lead. He had already given clear evidence of his ability to hold off tackles while waiting for reinforcements. This tactic was troubling Leeds and, in their apprehension, the rearguard allowed him the space to work a shooting position. He rode another tackle but then shot wide with only Sprake to beat.

At the start of the second half Madeley clashed heads with Marchetti. He had to be withdrawn on a stretcher and needed three stitches in a cut eye, Mick Bates replacing him.

The Italians exerted some dominance over the following quarter of an hour as they enjoyed a period of pressure. Leeds withstood the challenge, but their readiness even this early to settle for the draw that would secure the trophy was a little surprising.

Juventus had enough about them to sustain a forward threat and Sprake needed to be at his best to save a magnificent drive from Furino. However, the Italians also seemed reluctant to commit themselves fully to attack and were content to wait for Leeds to come out, seeking to catch them on the counter.

With fifteen minutes of the contest remaining, Salvadore was booked for scything down Cooper and a couple of minutes later there was more trouble. Cooper put a centre into the box and as Tancredi fell to the floor with the ball, Bates struck out as it ran loose. He accidentally kicked the keeper and was promptly set upon by a posse of protesting Italians, one of whom appeared to punch him. That was the signal for a mass fracas, but referee Rudi Glockner calmly restored order.

With both sides opting for caution, there were few openings of any real merit, suiting the Yorkshiremen down to the ground.

In the end, Leeds were simply too adept to be caught out by Juve's quick thoughts and movement. The Italians were superb in midfield but that was not enough against the strength and resilience of the United rearguard.

Juventus could not fashion another opening. The 1-1 draw at ninety minutes left the aggregate score at three apiece, with Leeds the victors by virtue of away goals.

It was hard luck on the Italians, who had gone through the entire competition without a defeat. Nevertheless, the rules had been clear from the start of the competition, and United had experienced enough heartache and near things over the years to afford too much sympathy for their opponents.

Billy Bremner and his men got a standing ovation from the crowd as they went up to collect the trophy. Bremner said:

> After all our disappointments of the past couple of seasons it was a great feeling showing off the Fairs Cup at the end … When I got that trophy in my hands, everything suddenly became worthwhile again. Gone was the feeling of frustration and despair we at Elland Road have felt so often. In its place was a sense of pride.
>
> I know it has been said that we could have attacked more than we did in the second half but we decided to play it a little safer in the second period. Italians are masters of breaking out of defence with devastating speed and accuracy and they had the forwards to cash in on such tactics. That is the way they play the game in Italy and that is the way they wanted to play it at Elland Road. They were dying for us to come at them. They stood back in defence waiting for us to surge forward and it was tempting. But had we done so we would have been suckers for the counter punch. So we declined the invitation to Fairs Cup suicide and sat back ourselves waiting for them to come. After all they needed a goal at that stage far more than we did. Six seasons in Europe have taught us plenty.

The shiny silver trophy that Bremner lifted at the end of the game was a tremendous compensation for their efforts. To have gone through a second successive campaign without any material reward would simply have been too much to bear. As it was, they could bask in the glory of another European triumph.

Elland Road
Attendance: 42,483

Leeds United: Sprake, Reaney, Cooper, Bremner, Charlton, Hunter, Lorimer, Clarke, Jones, Giles, Madeley (Bates)

Juventus: Tancredi; Spinosi, Salvadore, Marchetti, Furino, Morini, Haller, Capello, Causio, Anastasi, Bettega

33

Leeds United 5-1 Manchester United
First Division
19 February 1972

The antagonism between the two Uniteds of Leeds and Manchester is among the most bitter in English football. Most such rivalries are based on the desire for bragging rights between neighbouring clubs, but the Leeds-Manchester case is an entirely different ball game, with 40 miles and the entire Pennines dividing the two cities and a mutual loathing linking them.

Whites manager Don Revie had a deep and abiding respect for Matt Busby, the long-serving Old Trafford manager, seeking out his advice and guidance when he was first appointed boss at Elland Road.

Revie showed little of that respect, however, when he eagerly snatched Johnny Giles away from Manchester for a cut price fee in 1963 and converted him into one of the supreme midfield generals of the sixties and seventies, capitalising on one of Busby's rare errors of judgement.

Nine years on from the Giles transfer, Leeds United enjoyed one of their greatest triumphs over the Old Trafford club, even more satisfying because it marked the symbolic ending of the Reds' pursuit of the League title.

Manchester United had been early pace setters, topping the table from 9 October until the first week of January. By 19 February, when they faced Leeds at Elland Road, they had gone off the boil, without a League win since 4 December.

Revie's men had ended the unbeaten record of the Reds at Old Trafford with a 1-0 win at the end of October; the Whites could also boast good recent form with only a single defeat since 13 November.

Logic pointed to only one conclusion, but few anticipated what would happen on a day that will always be remembered with glee by Elland Road supporters.

The Whites could and should have been well clear by half-time. Leeds had pounded away at the Manchester defence, but the visitors somehow managed to reach the break without conceding; it looked just a matter of time before the floodgates opened.

Within two minutes of the resumption, the home crowd were roaring their glee.

Giles got the ball just outside the Reds' box and rolled it to Allan Clarke on the byline. He shaped to cross first time, throwing defenders Steve James and Tommy O'Neil off balance, before cutting inside and feeding Eddie Gray. The Scot turned smartly and his instant strike was touched onto the post by Stepney. The ball seemed to have crossed the goal line, but Jones was on it in a flash to make sure.

Seven minutes later, Leeds were two ahead. Tony Dunne's ball forward sold Bobby Charlton short and Giles took possession, passing long to the unmarked Lorimer coming in on the left. The Scot dropped his shoulder and rounded O'Neil on the outside to clip over a cross left-footed. It beat both Jack Charlton and Clarke in the middle and reached Jones who swept it goalwards. The shot left Stepney flat-footed, though the goal was awarded to Clarke for his barely perceptible flick.

In the fifty-seventh minute, the Reds hinted that they might be able to spring an undeserved comeback when Francis Burns knocked the ball in off a post following a free-kick.

But Leeds were not to be denied and within a minute had restored their two-goal advantage. Billy Bremner earned space on the right to loop a high cross to the far post. Jones rose to head the ball down and into the net with Stepney and his defenders starting the post-mortem.

The sixty-second minute brought a fourth. Gray rounded Dunne to find the byline on the right and flicked the ball back for Lorimer to fire across goal. Jones was there to touch the bobbling ball past Stepney and complete his hat-trick.

Still they were not satisfied and Lorimer grabbed a fifth after seventy-four minutes. Giles deftly curled a killer ball through the Manchester defence to find the tireless Jones running into space. The centre forward took it wide of his man and thumped it to the back post. The cross struck the thigh of the onrushing Lorimer and bounced back across goal. The Scot was first to the dropping ball and crashed it left-footed into the roof of the net.

In that first thirty minutes of the second half, Leeds had swept Manchester United away. As if sated by the flood of goals, Don Revie's men were content thereafter to play possession football. The ecstatic Elland Road crowd revelled unashamedly in the destruction of the hated visitors, deriding them mercilessly.

Elland Road
Attendance: 45,399

Leeds United: Sprake, Madeley, Cooper, Bremner, Charlton, Hunter, Lorimer, Clarke, Jones, Giles, E. Gray

Manchester United: Stepney, O'Neil, Dunne, Burns, James, Sadler, Morgan, Kidd (McIlroy), Charlton, Gowling, Best

34

Leeds United 7-0 Southampton
First Division
3 March 1972

Occasionally a match comes along that achieves legendary status; one such game in March 1972 saw Don Revie's Leeds United give the performance that would be cited forever as their coup de grace.

Southampton were struggling badly at the time and considered little more than cannon fodder for the Whites, who had been beaten only once since losing 2-1 to the same Saints side at the Dell on 13 November. The Hampshire team had managed a mere seven points from their twelve games since then. In the same period, United had dropped six points, scoring twenty goals and conceding five.

Southampton had their favoured strike pairing of Ron Davies and Mike Channon on show and it was the latter who got in the first shot of the game, a speculative effort from 20 yards easily gathered by Gary Sprake. From that moment on, Leeds dominated the proceedings and with seventeen minutes gone, they came close to an opening goal. When Billy Bremner fed a free-kick to Johnny Giles, the Irishman hammered a shot narrowly wide from the edge of the box.

The two diminutive schemers took firm control of midfield, keeping Southampton penned in their own half. The Leeds statement of intent was underlined by Sprake having only one shot to save in the first half hour.

The only element missing from United's performance was goals and with eight minutes of the first period remaining, they put that matter right. Bremner had the ball in the centre circle and with Eddie Gray haring past him at pace down the centre, the Scot laid it perfectly into his path. Gray prodded it forward to Mick Jones, stood on the edge of the area with his back to goal. Jones laid the return pass back to Gray, who hurdled a despairing tackle before finding Allan Clarke with a slide rule pass. The England striker flew into the space created by the killer ball, took it on one step into an acute angle and slammed his shot left-footed into the opposite corner.

That advantage was doubled within five minutes when Gray fed Peter Lorimer as the Scot broke down the right channel. He took the ball in his stride to hammer a low shot into the far corner.

There was no respite for Saints after the resumption. Gray, Lorimer and Clarke were constant thorns in Southampton flesh, refusing to give them a moment's peace. Lorimer headed wide from a Giles cross and then Gray cleared the bar from inside the 6-yard box with the goalkeeper helpless.

It could hardly be termed the calm before the storm, but certainly a tempest blew Southampton away in the eighteen minutes following the hour mark.

In the sixtieth minute, Giles had possession inside the centre circle and passed short to Bremner to his right. The Scot held it up long enough for Giles to make his break beyond him into space and then fed him with pinpoint accuracy. The Irishman took it on a couple of strides and then coolly slipped the ball through the Southampton defence for Clarke's cleverly timed run. The striker picked the ball up, cut across a defender, shifted the ball out from under his feet and passed it home left-footed for 3-0.

Reaney's 25-yard shot brought Martin to his knees before Leeds added their fourth after sixty-four minutes.

United were awarded a free-kick out wide on the right, but instead of lofting it across the box, Bremner slipped it short to Lorimer, who powered in a shot from the corner of the penalty area. The ball was blocked by a Saints defender deep inside the goal area and then cleared out to the left by O'Neil. As Jenkins sought to come away with it, Bremner was too quick and determined for him, and from behind lunged across the winger to win the ball for Giles. The playmaker was fouled by Stokes as he looked to make ground. Advantage was given and the ball ran on for Lorimer to pick up, dance past his marker and fire home from 20 yards.

Four minutes later it was Lorimer again with a carbon copy strike. Fry tried to clear the ball, but Lorimer intercepted and burst through the defence to complete his hat-trick.

The sixth goal, after seventy-three minutes, was the most remarkable score of the afternoon. United's centre backs had grown bored with confinement in their own half and both men moved forward. Norman Hunter danced out wide to the left byline and, like a natural winger, stood an inviting lobbed cross up to the back post. Jack Charlton had drifted up into the area and rose above everyone to nod the ball home. The goal got a special cheer from the Elland Road faithful as Big Jack loped back into his defensive position sporting a grin as wide as the Yorkshire moors.

Twelve minutes from time and it was 7-0. Gray hurdled a tackle on the left and sent over a cross, Lorimer nodded it back into the goal area and Jones pounced to sweep the ball over the line.

In truth, the goals were only a prelude to further humiliation for Southampton. United, seemingly bored with scoring, now played keep ball with an astonishing succession of flicks, twists and tricks: a back heel from Bremner here, a crossfield lob from Giles there, deft touches and turns everywhere, as the outclassed visitors were made to look like Sunday League amateurs.

It was later claimed that the antics were designed not to humiliate Southampton but simply to keep United's players clear of injury. It did not look that way at the time, however, as Leeds took on the role of adroit matadors, each seemingly intent on outdoing each other with every successive move.

Even when a pass seemed to have gone astray, a United man moved through the gears to recover the ball and feed it on to a colleague. Rarely has there been such a one-sided, arrogant display of possession football. This was ruthless, pitiless artistry as the rapier was plunged in and in again as hapless Southampton players tried in vain to get a touch over that final five minutes.

Bremner commented:

At half-time there was not a thought that we would turn our possession into so many goals. John Giles was playing out of his skin, every touch he made looked elegant and he was more like a ballet dancer that game so exquisite was his touch. As the game wore on I felt that my game moved to a new level, ball tricks I would normally only practice in training sessions appeared throughout the game. The boss was not one who enjoyed such antics from his players. He wanted more direct football, and finesse and trickery came after results as far as he was concerned. However, we enjoyed and milked every moment of it. It wasn't a deliberate attempt to make Southampton look inferior, it just happened that way.

Elland Road
Attendance: 34,275

Leeds United: Sprake, Reaney, Madeley, Bremner, Charlton, Hunter, Lorimer, Clarke, Jones, Giles, E. Gray

Southampton: Martin, McCarthy, Fry, Stokes, Gabriel, Steele, Paine (Byrne), Channon, Davies, O'Neill, Jenkins

35

Leeds United 1-0 Arsenal
FA Cup Final
6 May 1972

1972 marked 100 years since the first FA Cup final and United were only too pleased to be one of the combatants in the centenary final. The FA marked the occasion with a parade of all thirty-seven previous winners. Club flags were carried, followed by kitted out players, the number of whom signified how many times each club had been successful. Aston Villa, seven time winners, led the way, followed by Blackburn and Newcastle (six each); Leeds, without a win, were absent, but opponents Arsenal had four representatives.

Half an hour earlier, Don Revie announced a selection that saw David Harvey retain the goalkeeper's jersey in place of Gary Sprake.

The Gunners also fielded a deputy keeper, with Geoff Barnett covering for Bob Wilson, injured in the semi-finals.

The first five minutes of match action confirmed that the game would be competitive.

When Peter Lorimer looked to make progress, Bob McNab launched himself at the ball, but caught the man. Forty-eight seconds had passed since the kick-off and referee David Smith decided he had to lay down a marker. In close view of the Royal Box, Smith took the name of McNab to set a record for the earliest booking at Wembley.

Armstrong and Reaney threw themselves into a 50:50 challenge with their studs showing; Radford clashed with Hunter and then Storey hammered Giles as he tried to play the ball; Charlton threw himself into a huge lunge to prevent Graham's throw in reaching Radford. It was clear that neither defence would leave many holes and that midfield would be a fiercely contested area, with Storey doggedly hounding Giles, and Bremner and Ball never far from each other's side.

When Storey tried to settle on a throw midway in the Leeds half, Lorimer crashed in hard on him, surprisingly emerging with the ball. He set Gray loose on the left, but the winger was sent tumbling to earth by Storey's vengeful challenge. Referee Smith awarded United the kick and Madeley slipped the ball short to Giles, who fed Gray again on the left. Gray jinked inside Ball's desperate challenge but could do nothing when George clattered through him from behind. Leeds were awarded another free-kick, 10 yards outside the area. Gray looked resigned to his fate while George just smirked with satisfaction. After four minutes, there had already been five free-kicks with as many robust challenges going unchecked.

Reaney's loose header allowed George to start a move. A promising combination was ended, however, when the referee adjudged that Radford, with his back to goal, had obstructed Hunter behind him. The decision provoked a volley of insults from Radford towards Hunter, with the centre forward protesting vigorously that the defender had kicked through him. For a minute Hunter's eyes flashed angrily before he regained his normal affable composure.

Radford and Hunter continued to spar and when they jumped for a high ball after fifteen minutes Radford took exception to Hunter's swinging arm. The two men clashed again as they challenged for Barnett's long ball; the referee gave a free-kick to Hunter, which sparked some wry smiles from the pair.

Hunter was given a lecture for snapping at George's heels 30 yards from goal. He came away smiling, but the offence nearly brought the first goal. The ball was teed up for McLintock to run onto at pace and he fired in a tremendous low strike, which changed direction off the turf. It was heading in until Harvey dived to claim, albeit somewhat untidily.

Ball tricked Clarke on the halfway and was going past him before the striker's momentum took him through with the challenge. He was ticked off by the referee, denying Arsenal the quick free-kick they wanted and they conceded possession to Bremner when they restarted.

For all the United dominance, Arsenal almost scored after Charlton was forced to concede a corner after thirty-one minutes when Ball looked to play George in.

Armstrong took it from Arsenal's left and his floated ball dropped invitingly for Ball, lurking on the edge of the area. His drive was timed perfectly, the ball struck with the outside of his foot for the bottom corner. It is doubtful whether the little England international ever caught a ball more cleanly. As it curled unerringly towards its target, the ever-reliable Reaney showed tremendous reflexes to block it away.

In the final minute of the normal forty-five, United almost scored the goal the game needed.

Giles floated the ball over McNab to Gray on the right and his cushion header to Lorimer was perfect. Lorimer sought the quick one-two with Bremner but McNab misjudged his clearance as he fell, sending the ball up into the air. Lorimer adjusted his feet beautifully as he waited for it to drop and sliced an acrobatic power drive beyond the back post. The ever-alert Clarke stooped into a brilliant header from the corner of the goal area that dropped gently off the face of Barnett's crossbar and ran clear. It was a major escape for Arsenal.

As the game neared half-time, Bremner was the third name to go in the book as he argued with the referee about the award of a goal kick to Arsenal.

Leeds finished the half in the ascendant but Don Revie's hasty exit to the dressing room hinted that he was not overly confident.

George became the fourth man booked after throwing himself in frustration at Bremner after losing possession less than a minute after the resumption. A confrontation looked likely until Bremner saw the sense of compromise.

Clever combination work by Leeds down the right saw Clarke work with Reaney to feed Gray. He feinted to come inside, throwing Ball off balance, before sending over a low cross. The ball was deflected by Simpson over Barnett's head against his right-hand post and into the net. The whistle had already gone, however, for Gray was unable to catch the ball before it ran out.

In the fifty-fourth minute Leeds opened the scoring with a well-crafted goal.

Charlton coolly dispossessed George and Madeley went striding purposefully forward, feeding Lorimer who sent it on to Jones down the right channel. The centre forward stood McNab up before dropping his shoulder and rounding the full-back. The ball ran loose from McNab's attempted tackle, and Jones was quickly onto it. He sent an inviting centre beyond the penalty spot where Clarke was lurking. Sniffer threw himself forward, nodding the ball past Barnett and into the bottom corner as the United fans exploded into life. A truly memorable goal!

The goal added to Leeds' burgeoning confidence and they took on a dominant air as their supporters began chanting 'Super Leeds'.

Bremner barred Barnett's path, trying to force him to use his left foot as he sought to punt the ball clear. The Scot got a touch to the ball, flicking it over the keeper's head, but the referee awarded a free-kick to Bremner's mock indignation.

There was a testy incident after sixty-three minutes between Ball and Bremner. Charlton's hefty free-kick forward deep into the Arsenal box came back to the United skipper. He sought to keep possession on the touchline, holding the ball cleverly with his back to goal and Ball snapping at his heels. The Arsenal man struck three times at the Leeds captain from behind before finally losing his patience and hacking Bremner's legs from under him in a red mist of frustration. He then angrily tried to tug him to his feet. The referee gave Ball a lengthy talking to for his irritable assault but Bremner's sporting intervention probably saved the Arsenal man from being booked.

In the sixty-ninth minute Arsenal almost snatched an equaliser. Ball brought the Gunners forward, combining well with Graham before sending a shot in from 30 yards. It deflected off Giles' heels and fell nicely for George to reach across Reaney and crash the ball powerfully against the United bar as he fell. George had done precious little in the game, but it was a brilliant strike that almost brought an undeserved equaliser.

The shock jolted United out of any complacency that might have been emerging. Seemingly unperturbed, they responded by creating three excellent chances in as many minutes.

Hunter began a move with a splendid ball curled with the outside of his left foot to Bremner. The Scot worked patiently to develop the move but when he found Charlton with an accurate long pass, the defender surrendered possession with a poor ball. The Gunners looked to fashion another move but Hunter, playing the game of his life, beat George to it and then turned away from the onrushing Ball to get his men moving again.

Giles swept the ball out to Reaney, who combined well with Bremner before the captain fed Lorimer. Simpson, McLintock and McNab were all drawn towards the wide man, who had spotted an acre of open space between the Gunners rearguard and their penalty area; he arced the ball through for Gray to have a clear run on goal with only Rice barring his way. Gray dallied in possession as he sought to turn the full-back and McLintock had enough time to get back and ruin the shot when it finally came. It was a sad waste and the unmarked Clarke protested furiously at Gray's profligacy.

Hunter again showed his determination in the tackle as he came forward with the ball, and he sparked a period of good possession that saw Lorimer earn a corner on the right.

After eighty-seven minutes, Bremner won a ball he had no right to and gained possession for Giles, Clarke, Madeley and Gray to work all the way to the opposite wing and into the box for Jones, but Storey did enough to edge the ball back to Barnett.

An Arsenal corner seconds later was headed away by Charlton, and then Leeds recovered the ball to begin winding down the game with clever possession football.

With seconds remaining, Hunter broke up an attack for the umpteenth time, worked a one-two with Giles and sent Jones clear down the right channel. He made for goal, floored McLintock with neat footwork and bore down on Barnett. The keeper dived at his feet and Jones tumbled over, his left arm collapsed under him. He stayed down, obviously in great pain, the elbow dislocated.

That was the final meaningful action; after Charlton stooped low to head away a through ball, referee Smith blew his whistle to confirm that United had won the FA Cup.

It was one of the most iconic moments in the club's history as Billy Bremner took the trophy from the Queen, inspiring rousing cheers of triumph.

Bremner: 'It was a very proud moment when I raised the FA Cup above my head. No other Leeds captain had done that and to me it represented a lot of hard work by everyone connected with our club, including our brilliant supporters. I felt like saying, "Here it is! You've all won it!"'

Wembley Stadium
Attendance: 100,000

Leeds United: Harvey, Reaney, Madeley, Bremner, Charlton, Hunter, Lorimer, Clarke, Jones, Giles, E. Gray

Arsenal: Barnett, Rice, McNab, Storey, McLintock, Simpson, Armstrong, Ball, George, Radford (Kennedy), Graham

Wolverhampton Wanderers 2-1 Leeds United
First Division
8 May 1972

Two days after winning the FA Cup for the first time in their history, Leeds United had an outstanding opportunity to become League champions and completing the coveted double. The title would be United's should they avoid defeat at Molineux against Wolves. Mathematically, a draw by Leeds might allow third-placed Liverpool to sneak past them on goal average, but the Merseysiders would require an 11-0 victory at Arsenal. If Leeds lost, a Liverpool victory would see them win the title.

There was potentially a third scenario: if United lost and Liverpool failed to win, table-topping Derby County would be champions. However, that eventuality was considered too remote a possibility to seriously contemplate even by the Rams, with manager Brian Clough and his players having departed on their summer holidays.

United's Cup-winning elation had been cut short by a coach ride to Wolverhampton immediately after the game. Don Revie's attempts to get the Wolves fixture delayed had fallen foul of Football League secretary Alan Hardaker.

Already without Terry Cooper, missing with a broken leg, United had to do without Mick Jones, who had dislocated his elbow in the closing seconds at Wembley. In addition, Allan Clarke and Johnny Giles had painkilling injections before the game, and Eddie Gray and Clarke both played with heavy strapping. Jones' place was taken by Mick Bates, playing in midfield, with Billy Bremner operating up front.

United began as if they were determined there would be no slip up, though they had a moment of anxiety after five minutes when goalkeeper David Harvey came out to collect a Wolves free-kick. Veteran Wanderers striker Derek Dougan got to the ball first and headed down to John Richards, who shot powerfully from 8 yards out. Paul Madeley blocked it and then cleared the danger.

Billy Bremner had the first opening for United when Frank Munro slipped as he tried to clear; the Leeds captain also fell victim to the greasy surface as he attempted a spectacular overhead kick.

Soon afterwards Wolves keeper Phil Parkes collided with Clarke in the area and the visitors' appeals for a penalty seemed fully merited. They were even more emphatic in the twenty-fifth minute after Bremner's shot was blocked; the ball ran to Clarke on the edge of the area and when the England striker lobbed it back in defender Bernard Shaw seemed to get both hands to the ball to prevent the goal. Referee Bill Gow was unsighted with Shaw facing away from him, and the linesman offered little clarification.

United continued to press Wolves back, but they were in despair in the forty-third minute. Madeley was forced to concede a corner, Wolves' second of the night, while Leeds had managed seven. Winger Dave Wagstaffe took it short and Shaw's low diagonal cross was sliced into danger by Giles' attempted clearance. Munro's shot through a crowded area found the net via a post despite Reaney's attempt to block. You could sense the collective shudder in the Leeds ranks.

Don Revie worked his restorative magic during half-time and his men were immediately back on the offensive once the second period commenced. The pressure led to Jim McCalliog conceding a free-kick and the Scottish midfielder was booked when he felled the heavily limping Clarke as he sought to insinuate his way into Wolves' defensive wall.

Lorimer's driven free-kick from 30 yards was somehow scrambled away by Wolves, though there was suspicion of another handball by Shaw. The defender was cautioned soon afterwards.

United were now on perpetual attack, and goalkeeper Harvey had to make two excellent saves as they left gaps at their rear. But Leeds came close several times to an equaliser, with strikes in quick succession from Giles, Clarke and Clarke again all being saved by a diving Parkes. Clarke was booked for dissent during this period of pressure.

After sixty-seven minutes, however, Wolves doubled their lead. Hegan and Richards led a quick break and the latter's cross from the right was smartly despatched by Dougan, skilfully flicking it past Harvey.

The die was cast, and Revie was forced into one final gamble. He withdrew the struggling Clarke, summoned Yorath from the bench and pushed Bremner and Charlton forward. He must have regretted not making the call earlier as the decision paid instant dividends. Giles swung an immaculate pass out to the left, Madeley played it into the very heart of the Wolves area to give Bremner an opportunity. He needed no second bidding, smashing it emphatically into the roof of the net.

Gerry Taylor and Hegan were booked for Wolves and then Madeley had to clear a Wagstaffe shot off the line as United abandoned any pretence of defence. Then Richards lobbed the ball onto Harvey's bar from 15 yards. Undeterred, United pressed anxiously for the equaliser that could yet give them the championship.

They nearly got it at the death: Charlton lobbed the ball into the centre and Yorath nodded it over the head of goalkeeper Parkes from 6 yards, but couldn't get a meaningful touch. He claimed later that if he had managed to head the ball, he would have buried it but it only flicked his hair. Up popped Taylor to head the ball off the line as time seemed to stand still. The Leeds challenge was over.

Eric Todd in *The Guardian*:

This surely will go down as one of the bravest failures of all time. Indeed, I hesitate to call it a failure at all.

To what extent Leeds were affected by the mental and physical strain and euphoria of Saturday's FA Cup final may not be calculated. Nor shall we ever know whether Leeds would have earned the crucial point if Jones had been available. But in spite of all Fortune's mocking ... Leeds simply would not give in. As if to cock a snook at authority, which demanded that they should play a League game during Cup final week and another game two days after Wembley, Leeds were at their considerable best. And if Bremner has played a more inspired or inspiring game I wish I had seen it. He led the forward line as though he had been there all his playing life.

With Jones absent and Clarke not fully fit, even when the game started, Leeds could have been forgiven for aiming only for a draw. A draw, with Bremner directing operations? It was not to be contemplated. He drove his men as they never have been driven before and every single one of them responded magnificently.

It was not only the United players who had cause to bemoan the vagaries of refereeing decisions that night. Liverpool had to settle for a goalless draw at Highbury against Arsenal and Bill Shankly was enraged when Roger Kirkpatrick ruled out an eighty-eighth-minute goal by John Toshack for offside.

The two results left Brian Clough's Derby County as shock champions on fifty-eight points; Leeds, Liverpool and Manchester City (fourth) were all on fifty-seven in one of the most open championship races for years.

The Wolves-Leeds game would in later years assume enormous significance in the history of the club.

Stuart Sprake and Tim Johnson commented in *Careless Hands: The Forgotten Truth of Gary Sprake*:

> The *Sunday People* revealed that an attempt had been made to fix the game, with offers made to Wolves' players to throw the match. An inquiry was held but was to prove inconclusive as no evidence was found after a shroud of secrecy descended and no-one could identify Revie's agent or middle man.
>
> Five years later, during Richard Stott's investigation, the identity of the middle man was revealed. It was Mike O'Grady, the former Leeds winger, who was on Wolves' books at the time ... The investigating team confronted O'Grady, who admitted to being the go between. When questioned about the incident, he replied: 'It was me. No-one else was involved, just Revie and me. It was a one-to-one situation and I just did as I was asked and made an approach. I never received any money so I am not implicated, I never received a penny. It was suggested I go and see what the reaction would be, which I did but the Wolves player I spoke to said it was a no go.'
>
> According to the *Mirror* the player approached was Bernard Shaw, who promptly informed his manager, Bill McGarry. He in turn gathered the players together to warn them of the money that was perceived to be flying around and to be careful. The *Mirror* further alleges that during the match many appeals were made by Leeds' players to their opposite numbers to take it easy and to give away penalties. The winger Dave Wagstaffe was having an inspired game and cries from the touchline urged him to 'Take it easy, we'll see you right.' At the heart of the Wolves defence centre half Frank Munro was urged to concede a deliberate penalty. Four months after the game both Wagstaffe and Munro admitted to the *Sunday People* that attempts had been made to fix the game, although they both declined. Munro confirmed that he had two offers of large sums of money, one before and one during the game if he would give away a penalty.

As always with such affairs, there are two sides to this particular story; in the interests of objectivity, these are the facts and findings of the libel case brought by Billy Bremner against the *Sunday People* and Danny Hegan at the High Court in London.

The case concluded on 3 February 1982 with Bremner awarded damages of £100,000 after the jury decided that the *People* was not justified in its accusations. Hegan told a reporter and repeated in evidence that Bremner offered him £1,000 to give away a penalty in the Wolves game. Bremner denied that he had ever offered a bribe to a player or attempted to fix a match.

Bremner told the jury that he gave up his playing career because of terrace jibes at away matches that he had fixed games.

Evidence supporting Bremner was given by Johnny Giles, Jack Charlton, Allan Clarke and Derek Dougan. As a Wolves player and therefore ostensibly objective, Dougan's evidence was vital; he said he never heard any Leeds player, or anyone else connected with them, offer bribes. Giles said the allegations were 'ludicrous', while Charlton branded them 'total nonsense'.

Bremner's counsel asked for large damages to compensate the Scot for injury to his reputation and distress caused to him and his family.

The jury retired for two hours before finding in favour of Billy Bremner. The award of £100,000 was at the time one of the highest made in the High Court. The publishers, Odhams Newspapers, and Hegan were ordered to pay the damages plus the costs of the seven-day hearing, estimated to be more than £60,000.

Molineux
Attendance: 53,379

Wolverhampton Wanderers: Parkes, Shaw, Taylor, Hegan, Munro, McAlle, McCalliog, Hibbitt, Richards, Dougan, Wagstaffe

Leeds United: Harvey, Reaney, Madeley, Bremner, Charlton, Hunter, Lorimer, Clarke (Yorath), Bates, Giles, E. Gray

37

Leeds United 1-0 Wolverhampton Wanderers
FA Cup Semi-Final
7 April 1973

The FA Cup semi-final against Wolverhampton Wanderers in April 1973 was the sixth time United had progressed to that stage in the nine seasons since they returned to the First Division. In contrast, it was Wolves' first appearance in the last four since 1960.

Norman Hunter, Eddie Gray, Mick Bates and Gordon McQueen were all injured, though Don Revie left it until the latest possible moment before naming his eleven, and the veteran Jack Charlton, a month shy of his thirty-eight birthday, retained his place.

Wolves almost took the lead after four minutes. Kenny Hibbitt, brother of former Leeds midfielder Terry, split the United defence with a through ball for Powell. The teenager had to hit the ball first time and David Harvey, quickly off his line, dived to smother the effort.

Leeds were starting to build some forward momentum and Terry Yorath showed some nimble footwork down the left. Munro tried a short pass out of defence to Hibbitt but it wrongfooted the midfielder and Yorath was in swiftly to nick the ball away. He rounded Munro's desperate sliding tackle and flicked the ball past Hibbitt. While Yorath's mind was on crossing the ball, the Wolves man had clearly decided that enough was enough and carried on into a lunging foul with his studs up. He caught Yorath on the shin and sent him writhing in agony. Referee Pat Partridge had little option other than to dish out the first caution.

Just after the half hour, Parkin was raiding at pace down the left and fired a ball through for Wagstaffe to chase. The winger got to it just as it reached the byline, but his cut back was easily cleared by Madeley at the near post. Unfortunately, the move brought tragedy for Jack Charlton, who pulled up in pain with a torn hamstring. Despite lengthy treatment he had to go off, replaced by Joe Jordan. In a tactical reshuffle, Yorath took Charlton's place at centre back while Lorimer came deep to strengthen midfield.

The half-time break rekindled Wolves' spirits and they made a concerted effort to raise their game.

Paul Madeley had hurt his shoulder in an incident inside the game's first ten minutes and was playing in great discomfort; with one substitution already made, he was forced to soldier on. He carried his arm gingerly throughout, telling Yorath to look after Dougan so he could protect his limb.

Wolves had little answer to the waves of United attacks at this stage of the game and were starting to grow frustrated at being penned back. As the needle started to creep in, Clarke was caught in the face by Wagstaffe and then Dougan became the second Wanderers player to have his name taken when he kicked out in a packed Leeds area.

Bremner was playing a captain's game and was at the heart of everything United did. A determined 40-yard run saw him shrug off several fierce tackles before the move broke down as it neared goal.

Bremner earned a free-kick when he crashed into Wagstaffe on the right touchline and Lorimer lofted the dead ball to the edge of the area. Jordan got to it but his header seemed to be drifting harmlessly behind for a goal kick until Clarke took it upon himself to chase and catch it on the goal line. He sent it back to Cherry and the full-back drove the ball low towards the penalty spot. Jones collected the ball as it ran loose off a Wolves clearance and fed it back to Giles. The Irishman clipped it into the box and Bremner teed up a chance with a back header. Jordan looped a header from eight yards narrowly over Parkes' crossbar.

United were not to be denied and took the lead following a sixty-ninth-minute corner. Giles' inswinger was headed away but Lorimer hooked it over his head and back in from 30 yards. The falling ball was misjudged by both Hibbitt and Jones and dropped into space in the middle of the box. Bremner was lurking with intent and was on the chance in a trice, flashing in a fierce left-footed shot. It beat Parkes' dive and billowed the net.

Bremner's extraordinary knack of bagging vital semi-final goals had served United well once again; his goals had also been decisive in 1965 and 1970.

It was the first goal Wolves had conceded in their Cup run and they were not ready to throw in the towel just yet. They looked more dangerous and when Parkin fired the ball to the feet of Richards in the United area, the young striker wriggled smartly round Madeley to fire low past Harvey. Unfortunately for Wolves, the ball trundled against the inside of the far post and bounced back kindly to Harvey.

With fifteen minutes left, Wolves boss Bill McGarry brought Mike Bailey on for Hibbitt as his final throw of the dice.

In the closing stages Yorath's long ball allowed Jordan to burst between tiring Wolves defenders and race into the penalty area. He seemed to have taken it too far as Parkes came out to face him down, but the ball ran on and from virtually on the byline, Jordan cut it back low right across the face of goal and beyond the far post. The Scot hung his head in frustration.

Still there was sufficient time for a dangerous Wolves free-kick, taken by Bailey from near the right touchline. Dougan met it perfectly with a flicked header, but it crept fractionally around Harvey's left-hand post as the keeper stood flat footed. But that was enough. The Wanderers had no more time and referee Partridge blew his whistle to signal that Leeds had reached their third FA Cup final in four seasons. Bremner said of it:

We've played together for so long that we take everything in our stride ... When Big Jack Charlton went off after half an hour, we didn't even have to look for instructions to the trainer's box, we all knew instinctively what could be done and we did it. You get this by playing together and there's no doubt our experience served us well against Wolves.

But I don't mind admitting my heart was in my mouth when Richards hit the post. I was on my knees practically nibbling at the grass.

Maine Road
Attendance: 52,505

Leeds United: Harvey, Reaney, Cherry, Bremner, Charlton (Jordan), Yorath, Lorimer, Clarke, Jones, Giles, Madeley

Wolverhampton Wanderers: Parkes, Taylor, Parkin, Shaw, Munro, McAlle, Powell, Hibbitt (Bailey), Richards, Dougan, Wagstaffe

38

Leeds United 0-1 Sunderland
FA Cup Final
5 May 1973

One of the lowest points in United's history came when they defended the FA Cup they won in 1972. The hottest favourites for years, Leeds were considered certainties to beat rank outsiders Sunderland. A day that should have been one of celebration ended instead in a trough of despair as Don Revie fell foul of an old enemy.

The grudge harboured by Sunderland boss Bob Stokoe had festered since 1962 when, he maintained, Revie had attempted to bribe him to throw a match when he was Bury player-manager. Stokoe was determined to have his vengeance and launched a masterclass in public relations to undermine United, as outlined by Rob Bagchi and Paul Rogerson in *The Unforgiven*:

> Bob Stokoe had free rein to begin an unsubtle but effective bout of psychological warfare against his opposite number. His first outburst was the usual nonsense about the allocation of 'England's dressing room', which had gone to United, and the matter of having the Leeds fans at the tunnel end, where the teams would enter the stadium ... Rather than dismissing or simply ignoring Stokoe's absurd gripe, Revie unwittingly revealed that it had fed his neurosis, commenting wearily that, 'We get blamed for practically all it is possible to get blamed for these days.' Wolves manager Bill McGarry's attack of sour grapes gave Stokoe more ammunition, as he declared himself 'staggered', in the aftermath of his side's semi-final defeat, 'at the way Bremner went the whole 90 minutes disputing every decision that went against his team'. 'I am not trying to knock Leeds in any way,' agreed a disingenuous Stokoe, 'but we are playing a real professional side and, let's face it, the word professionalism can embrace a multitude of sins as well as virtues. The case about Bremner is the only comment I want to make about Leeds. My message is simple. I want Mr [Ken] Burns, the Cup Final referee, to make the decisions and not Mr Bremner.'

Stokoe did his job well: Sunderland were supremely motivated, determined not to let their illustrious opponents settle.

Early on, Mick Jones was fractionally short of getting a vital touch as Peter Lorimer's low, driven free-kick sped across the face of goal. But Sunderland refused to be overawed and it was they who had the first shot in anger after twelve minutes. Billy Hughes sought to round off a fluent passing movement with a strike from 20 yards but his effort flew high and wide.

Hunter brought Leeds back onto the attack with an incisive run which took him to the Sunderland area. He took on Black Cats skipper Bobby Kerr at the byline and managed to get in a cross towards the near post. Lorimer attempted a flicked volley from an acute angle, but the ball flew wide.

Leeds pressed again, with Madeley spearing a beautiful through ball towards Clarke near the penalty spot. As the striker was turning to get in his shot, Dave Watson came flying in to deflect the ball away.

Minutes later Clarke's name was the first to go into the referee's book after he felled Hughes from behind. After twenty-four minutes, it seemed Hunter might follow suit when he kicked out wildly at Tueart. The Sunderland wide man needed treatment to his injured shins but Hunter escaped without a caution.

If those incidents hinted that the game might descend into violence, there was little else to concern the referee.

United were rocked to their foundations after thirty-five minutes when Sunderland took the lead from their first corner of the game.

A smooth Sunderland passing movement gave Kerr the space for an impudent chip from range, which came plopping down under David Harvey's bar. With Hughes racing in, the keeper opted for safety and tipped the ball over his crossbar.

United's preoccupation with Watson's aerial threat was their undoing. Hughes sailed the flag kick out to the far post where Watson was waiting, policed by Madeley and Jones. In the eventuality, the ball beat all three of them and sailed on to bounce off the chest of the incoming Vic Halom. It fell nicely for Porterfield in the centre of the area. He cushioned it on his thigh and stroked in a lovely volley. It was down the throat of Harvey, but the effort was simply too true and at too close a range to be denied. As if in symbolic surrender, Harvey was rooted with upraised arms as the shot clipped Clarke's shoulder on its way into the roof of his net.

Sunderland were ahead!

United were forced to soak up more pressure as the interval dawned, though they fashioned some pressure of their own. Lorimer had two shots blocked, one by a defender and the second by Montgomery.

It was all hands to the pump for a period as United stoked up the pressure in the Sunderland area, but there was always a man in red and white stripes throwing himself into the challenge.

Half-time came with Sunderland still ahead and with every reason to be proud of their first half display.

United had been unable to get a midfield grip but they restarted with a renewed sense of purpose.

Bremner made space for himself on the edge of the Sunderland box after forty-nine minutes, wrongfooting Pitt with a lovely drag back. He flashed in a left-footed shot that came back off the goalkeeper but there was no Leeds player close enough to capitalise.

United continued to exert pressure and Cherry had the ball in the net a minute later. Bremner lofted a free-kick into the Sunderland six-yard box and when Montgomery rose to claim the centre, Clarke barged into the keeper, causing him to drop the ball. Cherry was on hand to poke home the loose ball, but Leeds celebrations were rudely ended when the effort was disallowed.

They were also denied what seemed a blatant penalty in the fifty-sixth minute when Watson looked to have tripped Bremner, but, as Geoffrey Green noted in *The Times*,

'Perhaps Bremner's own past told against him instinctively as the referee dismissed the swift passage with an imperious wave of the arm.'

After sixty-five minutes came the moment when realisation dawned on United that this was simply not to be their day. The ball was worked from Hunter on the left to Giles and then Jones on the edge of the Sunderland box. His back to goal, he held play up before sliding the ball to Reaney in the deep. The full-back's lofted cross to the far post found Cherry coming in for a diving blind side header. Somehow, Montgomery got to it and palmed across the face of goal.

Lorimer moved in with a gaping goal in front of him, no more than 5 yards out, and struck his shot well and on target. 'And Lorimer makes it one-each!' was the assured summation of BBC commentator David Coleman.

Except he hadn't...

Montgomery had scrambled to his feet and hurled himself instinctively at the shot, somehow turning it up onto the underside of his crossbar and out. The prostrate Cherry flicked an involuntary leg at the ball, as if in mute protest at the lack of justice, but it ran away to be cleared.

Cherry beat the ground in frustration, Lorimer looked around in disbelief and a nation held its breath ... this was the stuff of dreams. Or nightmares, in United's case.

United were not yet ready to surrender, however, and pushed more men forward as their sense of urgency increased. Cherry was on almost permanent attack, while Madeley took every opportunity to throw his weight behind the forwards.

With fifteen minutes to go, United brought on Yorath for Gray. He was no match winner, but Revie gambled that his robust determination would serve Leeds better than Gray's somewhat insipid forays. The Welshman was involved almost immediately in the move that led to Cherry drawing another good save from Montgomery, as he came in for another diving header on the blind side.

United threw everything into attack as the clock ran down and Madeley had an angled shot stopped on the line. But Sunderland, having fought so well, were in no mood to surrender their advantage.

With two minutes remaining and United committed to kitchen sink aggression, there was a breakaway from Sunderland. They had a four on two advantage, but it looked like the move had broken down when Tueart could only find Madeley as he sought to play a killer through ball. But Hughes robbed the United man to revive the move and Halom, socks down around his ankles, had two shots from the edge of the Leeds box. Harvey leaped heroically to turn aside the second and better effort.

Sunderland had the ball in the Leeds net deep into injury time when Halom clumsily barged Harvey over the line, but the effort was disallowed. The incident ate up valuable seconds for Leeds, and they had no time to fashion another opportunity.

On raced Bob Stokoe, raincoat flapping, in a joyous sprint to embrace his heroic goalkeeper in one of the most memorable moments in Wembley history. The no hopers had won the Cup and Leeds' ambitions were dead in the water.

Billy Bremner commented:

Sunderland were determined not to let us settle. They chased and chased and chased. They concentrated on breaking up the partnership between Mick Jones and Allan Clarke and they were successful. Jimmy Montgomery was in brilliant form and has gone down in football history for one fantastic double save he pulled off ... I think we knew then that we were never going to score ... When Montgomery saved like that we didn't stop trying, but I think we all felt that it was not going to be our day.

It was a momentous day for Leeds United, catching them at a low and Sunderland at an irrepressible high, but it was far more symbolic than that: the determined young men of Revie's Golden Age had grown into weary, ageing troops and next to the vibrancy of Sunderland they looked like shadows of their former selves. In fact, it felt almost like Sunderland were the new Leeds, callow young men from the depths of the Second Division, unsettling higher class opponents, as Revie's kids had done a decade earlier.

United were not finished, as some critics gleefully claimed, and would come again, but on this particular day it felt like their time had passed.

Wembley Stadium
Attendance: 100,000

Leeds United: Harvey, Reaney, Cherry, Bremner, Madeley, Hunter, Lorimer, Clarke, Jones, Giles, E. Gray (Yorath)

Sunderland: Montgomery, Malone, Guthrie, Horswill, Watson, Pitt, Kerr, Porterfield, Halom, Hughes, Tueart

39

Leeds United 3-1 Everton
First Division
25 August 1973

The opening day of the 1973/74 season brought Everton to Elland Road. Ironically, in the closing days of the previous campaign, the Merseysiders had made United manager Don Revie what they thought was an offer he could not refuse when they settled on him as the man to revive their sagging fortunes.

The *Yorkshire Evening Post* reported that a contract worth £250,000 was on offer, including a tax free £50,000 golden hello. Such sums represented a small fortune when set against Revie's basic package of £17,500.

Revie eventually decided to stay at Elland Road, turning down other lavish offers from Panathinaikos and the Greek FA.

Now, as United set off on a new campaign, determined to prove they were not the spent force that many critics had eagerly claimed, the vagaries of the fixture lists brought the two clubs together.

The Everton side was a pale shadow of the outfit that had lifted the championship in 1970, but Howard Kendall, Colin Harvey and Joe Royle provided links with the glory days.

For Leeds, the giant Scot Gordon McQueen was given the opportunity to stake a claim as successor to the retired Jack Charlton.

The new corner stand at Elland Road was in full use for the first time and there was a crowd of 39,325 to watch as United began their tenth successive season in the First Division, their shirts bearing the iconic LU Smiley badge for the first time.

Only three minutes and forty-two seconds had elapsed when United received material reward for some early pressure when Billy Bremner opened the scoring.

Paul Madeley and Johnny Giles brought the ball forward smoothly out of their own half with a series of interchanges before Giles slipped the ball to Allan Clarke. The lanky striker made 20 yards before feeding a well-advanced Bremner, who tried to return to Clarke. The ball ran loose and the move seemed to have foundered as Bremner stumbled as he took on two men on the edge of the area. But, refusing to give way, he was much too fast for the Everton rearguard and as Clarke played the loose ball into space Bremner was up as quickly as he had fallen. He artfully flicked his way free to the left of three Everton defenders and thundered the ball home from 12 yards. It was a tremendous goal.

The United pressure intensified with goalkeeper David Lawson saving bravely at Lorimer's feet and then gathering a shot from Mick Jones. There was another close thing after twenty-four minutes when Madeley drew the Everton keeper well out of his station, took the ball around him and pulled a cross back across goal. Clarke sped in to take advantage, but Colin Harvey beat him to the ball and cleared.

This pattern continued unabated to the break, though there were no further goals. For all their first-half dominance, United's advantage was slender. There was thus a touch of anxiety when Everton showed some promise at the start of the second period. McQueen and Hunter had to work hard to keep them at bay, with the Merseysiders having three corners in rapid succession.

But Leeds now got their second wind, doubling their advantage on the hour mark.

They were given a free-kick out on the left flank, 40 yards from goal. Hunter tapped the ball to Gray, who took the ball inside before laying it back for Giles. The Irishman launched himself into a strike from 30 yards with the outside of his right foot; the ball arced beneath Lawson's despairing drive and just inside his right-hand post.

Five minutes later, it was 3-0.

Bremner, 40 yards out, swept a low ball through to Clarke just outside the area. The England front man side-footed it on to strike partner Jones, who took immediate advantage. He showed brilliant footwork to flick the back inside, over the head of his marker, and stab it past the advancing Lawson. It was another outstanding goal.

The score ended the game as a contest, despite Everton's refusal to give in. Thirteen minutes from time they gained some consolation, Joe Harper making it 3-1.

There was never a hint of anything like a revival and United saw out the game with their lead intact.

'Considering it was our first match, we played well,' said Bremner. 'We did not tear up any roots in our pre-season matches, but the atmosphere was ready made for us on Saturday, and considering it was our first match we played well. But I believe we can play better.'

The game was devoid of bookings, a heartening start to Revie's quest to improve United's disciplinary behaviour, but what most delighted Revie was the way his players put a lie to the claims of the critics that they were in decline, over the hill and washed up.

Elland Road
Attendance: 39,325

Leeds United: Harvey, Reaney, Madeley, Bremner, McQueen, Hunter, Lorimer, Clarke, Jones, Giles, E. Gray

Everton: Lawson, McLaughlin, Darracott, Lyons, Kenyon, Kendall, Harvey, Harper, Royle, Buckley, Connolly

40

Tottenham Hotspur 0-3 Leeds United
First Division
1 September 1973

It was in a mood of burgeoning self-confidence that United arrived at White Hart Lane after two wins from their opening two games, defeating Everton and following up with their first Division One victory in London since January 1971 by beating Arsenal at Highbury.

In addition to his aim of an unbeaten season, United manager Don Revie had promised that his team would improve their onfield behaviour after receiving a suspended £3,000 fine by an FA Disciplinary Commission, which ruled they had 'persistently violated the laws of the game and brought the game into disrepute.'

Revie responded by setting out his plans:

> I am very personally concerned, along with our directors, about our conduct record, and as manager am going to do everything in my power to make sure that this record is vastly improved by the end of the 1973/74 season.
>
> I have already told our players that it is up to myself and them to help the referee from now on and in every way we can by not talking to them or the linesmen and by not getting any unnecessary bookings.

Thus far, United had been true to Revie's words. While the Arsenal game had been keenly competitive, there had been none of the bitterness that had characterised the previous clash between the two sides at Highbury.

Leeds were unchanged, after Billy Bremner, Paul Reaney and Allan Clarke recovered from injuries sustained at Highbury.

United were quickly into their stride, opening the scoring after four minutes. A week earlier Bremner had netted at the same point against Everton and now repeated the feat.

It was a central thrust of Revie's plan for an increased attacking threat that the Scot should feature further upfield than normal and he quickly demonstrated his value in and around the box.

United had worked an attacking position on the edge of the Tottenham area and when Clarke sought to control the ball with his back to goal, defender Phil Beal bundled into him to concede a cheap free-kick. Peter Lorimer drove the dead ball, head high, to the edge of the 6-yard box. Spurs full-back Ray Evans and his skipper Martin Peters, each thinking the other was marking Bremner, left a yawning chasm between them.

Evans misjudged the flight of the ball, allowing it to clear his leap, and there was no danger that Bremner would fail to take full advantage. He powered home the inviting cross, giving Pat Jennings no chance as it flew over his upturned hands and in at the near post.

The visitors threatened again a few moments later, Eddie Gray firing over, but United went close to conceding a goal shortly afterwards following a corner kick.

The flag kick was cut back and when the cross flew into the area, Dillon dived to get in a good effort. Leeds keeper David Harvey managed to get a hand to the ball and Reaney completed the clearance from the line.

As if to reprimand Spurs for their impertinence, United quickly snapped back to double their advantage after fourteen minutes.

Tottenham sensed no danger as Lorimer carried forward, anticipating that he would build slowly with a pass to the overlapping Paul Reaney. Instead, the wide man drove a low ball through the Spurs defence towards Bremner running through to the edge of their area. It was a perfectly weighted through ball and the Scot did not have to check his stride as he caught it first time to stroke a curling effort into the corner.

That two-goal salvo visibly shook the home ranks but they retained at least a modicum of fight and managed to exert some pressure as Peters fired narrowly wide of Harvey's goal.

But the result seemed a foregone conclusion when Clarke opened his account for the season in the twenty-eighth minute.

Giles toyed with Cyril Knowles on the right, feinting a couple of times before artfully curling a pass down the touchline for Bremner in an advanced role. The United captain combined in splendid style with Lorimer, setting things up by cushioning the ball back for the wide man. There was a smart give and go and Bremner's accurate reverse pass sent Lorimer away down the line and he fired a cross through the heart of the Spurs box. Jones dived and missed but the ball ran on to the back post where Clarke gathered and coolly swivelled to hammer into the roof of the net.

Tottenham had shown little as an attacking force but they had a couple of opportunities shortly before half-time. Dillon saw his effort scooped off the line by the ever-watchful Reaney and then supplied the cross for Alan Gilzean, in the right place close in. The Scottish veteran rarely figured on a disappointing afternoon and provided more evidence that this was not to be his day when he fluffed the opportunity.

United might have been excused for sitting on their lead after the break, but they restarted in urgent fashion. Giles forced a corner in the opening minute and then Lorimer tried his luck with a 30-yard drive, which was comfortably pulled down by Jennings.

After that, United were content to absorb what pressure Spurs could muster and relied on intermittent breakaways to keep Jennings occupied.

Paul Madeley and Norman Hunter did sterling work in United's defence, but when Spurs made their late bid for consolation goals, no one was more to be praised than Paul Reaney and David Harvey.

There were no further goals at either end and United secured an impressive 3-0 triumph, which left them clear at the top of the table.

Barry Foster said in the *Yorkshire Post*:

With Billy Bremner looking like a new man and the new image of being the gentlemen of the League already accepted in most quarters, Leeds United sit politely at the top of Division One this morning, not only having demolished Tottenham Hotspur last Saturday but having won over their most critical observers in recent times – the London spectators.

In fact everything is going well just now for Leeds. They aimed to let their middle men give even more support to the strikers and Bremner, showing the zest and speed of their title year five seasons ago, has responded with three goals in as many games. They wanted to show they can still be the most attractive of teams and not get involved in trouble and twice in London last week, where previously they had found little success and a great deal of abuse, they produced faultless displays.

'We are getting on with the game and not getting involved in incidents,' said Bremner, who a week earlier had started the downfall of Everton with a quick goal. On Saturday he was at it again ... Two goals in ten minutes on a ground on which they had not found the net for over three years, and both from Bremner.

Geoffrey Green wrote in *The Times*:

Bremner and Giles as usual were the Leeds puppet masters. They designed the schemes and put them into effect, backed by a team who were complete in their instinctive understanding. Just when they ought to be growing a little rusty – in terms of time and heavy commitments over recent seasons – they are playing better than ever.

Up till half-time, Leeds provided a flawless exhibition. Bremner, quickly spotting the holes left by Dillon, constantly made advanced forays; Giles put his subtle stamp on the overall pattern, a little man with apparent endless time and space in which to work.

Even with just three games gone of the forty-two-match season, it was abundantly clear that the team to beat in the battle for the League championship would be this slick and authoritative United eleven.

White Hart Lane
Attendance: 42,801

Tottenham Hotspur: Jennings, Evans, Knowles, Coates, Dillon, Beal, Gilzean, Perryman, Chivers, Peters, Neighbour

Leeds United: Harvey, Reaney, Madeley, Bremner, McQueen, Hunter, Lorimer, Clarke (Cherry), Jones, Giles, E. Gray

41

Scotland 2-1 Czechoslovakia
World Cup Qualifier
26 September 1973

Scotland had qualified for the World Cup finals in both 1954 and 1958, but their following three attempts were abortive; when the draw for the 1974 finals put them in a group with Czechoslovakia and Denmark, hopes were high that they could end their exile.

For Billy Bremner, who featured in the unsuccessful qualifying campaigns in 1966 and 1970, it was a final shot at World Cup glory.

Scotland went into the game against the Czechs at Hampden in great heart, leading the group by a point after defeating the Danes twice. The visitors had a superior goal difference after beating Denmark 6-0 in June, but had dropped a point in the first game in Copenhagen a month earlier. A Scottish victory at home would see them through.

Bremner's Leeds teammate Peter Lorimer had scored the crucial second goal in the 2-0 victory at home to Denmark, but was unavailable against Czechoslovakia after being dismissed later in that game. The side was much changed with only Bremner and Kenny Dalglish remaining; manager Willie Ormond gave debuts to Tommy Hutchison and George Connelly, while the veteran Denis Law was recalled after an absence of fifteen months.

Czechoslovakia went into the game with a defensive mindset, gambling that they could overturn Scotland on the break. Their overtly physical approach saw Dalglish and Hutchison both fouled inside a minute. The referee was forced to speak to several of the Czechs before his patience gave way after nine minutes when he dished out a caution for a foul on Bremner that seemed no more deserving than those that preceded it.

Scotland were no saints themselves, with Law and Hay launching into blood curdling challenges and after twenty-one minutes the Czechs were forced to bring on Dobias for Kuna.

Bremner: 'It was another physical game. The Czechs started it. They came to defend at all costs and within the first few minutes both Kenny Dalglish and Tommy Hutchison were felled harshly. Someone also took my legs away and got booked for it. I then tackled someone else a bit hard just to let them know that we would not be standing for that sort of nonsense.'

Willie Morgan and Hutchison threatened much, while Bremner and Davie Hay dominated midfield. Law and Dalglish gave the Czechs plenty to worry about as they combined with Morgan, Hutchison and Bremner in quickfire pass-and-move thrusts.

John Downie in *The Times*:

The Czechoslovaks fell back as quickly as they advanced. There were few loopholes to be found once their defence mustered, and when a Scot did get in a shot he still had the acrobatic Viktor to contend with. Yet all the indications were that if a goal came it would be for Scotland.

So it was understandable that the full-throated roar of the noisiest Hampden Park crowd for some time was replaced by a contrasting hush when Czechoslovakia took the lead out of the blue in 33 minutes. A Scottish attack of lightning-fast short passes, involving Dalglish, Law, Hay and Bremner, had just been repulsed when Adamec sent a long diagonal pass to the right, where Nehoda met the ball first time with his boot and lobbed it into the far side of Scotland's goal. Hunter was so surprised that he neither moved out to narrow the angle nor got off the ground in what was more of a despairing flop than a dive to his right. The silence could be felt.

Scotland's push for an equaliser was rewarded five minutes before the interval. The Czech keeper was forced to touch a Law free-kick past his post at full length, but could do nothing when centre half Jim Holton buried Hutchison's resulting corner with a brutal header.

Scotland pressed on for the lead after the break and just past the hour Willie Ormond summoned Joe Jordan from the bench to replace the tiring Dalglish. The target man brought punch to the attack and took just eleven minutes to pierce the Czech defence.

Zlocha obstructed Law just outside his own area and Morgan touched the indirect free-kick to Bremner. The Scotland captain's shot struck the post but the rebound was captured by Morgan and his immediate centre was bulleted home by Jordan's header.

There were no further goals and Scotland were fully worthy of the victory. They were through to the World Cup finals in West Germany.

John Downie:

Here, at last, was a Scottish team who, faced by opponents who were as skilful as they were ruthless, kept hasty retaliation to a couple of isolated incidents, maintained the tempo that eventually ran the legs off the Czechoslovaks, and still concentrated in playing football that was a revelation in its variety and skill. Even the dispiriting loss of a soft goal after they had attacked without reward for most of the first thirty-three minutes did not disturb the constructive pattern.

For this, much praise must go to Bremner, a captain who protested heatedly to the referee about the treatment his players were receiving, but still maintained order and kept his team concentrating on the scoring of goals.

It was a momentous triumph for Bremner and his fellow Scots, as recalled by Joe Jordan:

I was twenty-one and I had no real sense of all that yearning and frustration felt by so many players I had idolised as a boy ... I could see on the faces of Law and Bremner that so much of the history of Scottish football, and their own lives, had gone into the game against the Czechs, which circumstances had given me the chance to influence. As the night wore on, the meaning of the victory, and the goal I had scored to create it, began to seep home.

Something else I noted in Glasgow, and when I thought about it I could see that it was all to do with the pain caused by the long Scottish absence from the World Cup finals, was Billy's determination to get back to Elland Road as soon as possible. There was no question of missing the first flight home to Leeds. The boys were already in training when we arrived, and Billy and I had a bath and a rub-down and we were waiting as they came in from their work. I could see how much Billy had wanted that moment, and how much pleasure and satisfaction he was gaining from it ... Bremner wanted that morning to proclaim with his physical presence that at last the Scots had made it. An important part of world affairs had been put right.

Hampden Park
Attendance: 89,028

Scotland: Hunter, Jardine, McGrain, Bremner, Holton, Connelly, Morgan, Hay, Law, Dalglish (Jordan), Hutchison

Czechoslovakia: Viktor, Pivarnik, Samek, Zlocha, Bendl, Bicovsky, Panenka (Capkovic), Kuna (Dobias), Adamec, Nehoda, Stratil

42

Hibernian 0-0 Leeds United
UEFA Cup: Second Round, Second Leg
7 November 1973

It could not have been clearer that the sights of Don Revie in the 1973/74 campaign were set on just one aim: regaining the championship.

United had finished runners up three times in the four seasons since their first title success in 1969 and Revie was determined that their pursuit would be successful this time.

When the Whites lost to Ipswich in the League Cup in October, the team was missing six internationals and two other regulars. It was obvious that trophies other than the big one were just a distraction.

There was a similar story in the UEFA Cup. After a 1-1 draw against the part-timers of Stroemsgodset, United fielded several reserves in the second leg as Revie sought to keep his men fresh for their title chase. Nevertheless, they won the game at a 6-1 canter.

United were paired with Hibernian in the second round. Again, Revie omitted five first teamers for the goalless first leg at Elland Road.

A 4-1 win against West Ham immediately before the second leg extended United's unbeaten League run to fourteen games; it did, however, leave Revie bemoaning a host of injuries with Harvey, McQueen, Hunter, Giles, Madeley and Jones unavailable to travel to Edinburgh, along with long-term absentees Eddie Gray and Cooper.

With Gary Sprake now in Birmingham's ranks, and his replacement, David Stewart, unavailable under UEFA's rules, Revie selected nineteen-year-old John Shaw in goal with rookie Glan Letheren (seventeen) as back up.

Also called into the party for the Easter Road clash were twenty-year-old Jimmy Mann, Sean O'Neill (twenty-one), Peter Hampton and Gary Liddell (both eighteen), with five appearances between them. In the eventuality, none of the four made it onto the pitch, but Roy Ellam, Terry Yorath, Joe Jordan, Mick Bates and Frank Gray started in the stead of more illustrious colleagues.

Among all the chopping and changing, Revie made one master stroke, opting to play Billy Bremner as sweeper, forsaking his captain's attacking abilities for the coolness he could bring to the rearguard. It was to prove a wise decision.

Hibs quickly pressed United back, skipper Pat Stanton, scorer of a hat-trick in their previous game, leading the assault on John Shaw's goal.

Jim Black went close in the opening minutes and then Alex Cropley threatened. In the tenth minute, defender John Blackley tore through the middle to unleash a tremendous swerving effort. Goalkeeper Shaw was equal to it, saving brilliantly.

After twenty-five minutes United came the nearest yet to breaking the deadlock from their first corner of the night. Frank Gray swung a low ball into the centre for Terry

Yorath to flick on. Roy Ellam was swiftly onto the opening and hammered in a shot, only to see it come back off the underside of the bar.

The game was hotting up, with the pressure on Shaw intensifying, but the young keeper was enjoying the game of his life. However, he sustained a hand injury just before the interval and was withdrawn, with Revie sending on the untried Letheren as replacement.

There are differences of opinion about Shaw's removal. It was claimed in some quarters that broken fingers in his right hand required strapping up, though more cynical commentators maintained that it was a ploy.

There were fears that the inexperienced Letheren might be found wanting under pressure, but he was soon performing heroics and Bremner marshalled the defence superbly, limiting Hibs' opportunities of testing the young Welshman.

Bremner was lauded afterwards for what many, including the home fans, acclaimed as the best defensive display ever seen at Easter Road. In one memorable incident, he back heeled the ball along his own goal line with two home forwards bearing down on him. This was a man at the top of his game, claiming later that he found the role of sweeper incredibly easy.

Gordon had the ball in the net for Hibs from a Stanton pass, but the effort was disallowed for offside. Then Letheren was penalised for taking too many steps but the indirect free-kick was repelled with some ease.

Hibs finished the game the stronger but clever defensive play by Bremner and Reaney extracted United from bother as the Scots threatened to take complete control. Bremner headed a Black header off the line before a 30-yard drive by Cropley skimmed the bar.

Despite many near things, the game failed to produce a goal, even after thirty minutes extra time. In the added time, United came close to settling things when Ellam put the ball in the net from a centre by Clarke, but the referee decided he had used his hand to control the ball.

The result mirrored that of the first leg at Elland Road, leaving the outcome to be settled by the drama of a penalty shoot out.

Hibernian won the toss to determine the order and it was Pat Stanton who was the first to try his luck.

Bremner knew Stanton well as a Scotland colleague and as he stepped up to take his penalty, Bremner sniped, 'You do realise that the whole of Scotland is looking at you?'

The mind games worked: Stanton crashed his effort against the post with Letheren beaten.

Lorimer followed for Leeds and made no mistake. Neither, in fact, did the seven men who followed, with Cropley, Blackley, Des Bremner and Hazel converting for Hibs and Gray, Bates and Clarke doing likewise for United. That left Bremner with the final spot-kick to settle the contest.

He was never going to miss after the performance he had given, slotting home off the underside of the crossbar to decide an enthralling tie.

Geoffrey Green in *The Times*:

This had been a golden night for [Bremner] with a performance of cool, deadly skill, spiced with arrogance which, as it were, thumbed a nose at all his brothers north of the border ... They were served by two novice goalkeepers – the first, Shaw, who retired at half-time and whose fingers of his right hand were later strapped together and may well have been broken. In his place came Letheren, and he was the second hero of the night behind Bremner, with at least four dazzling saves as Hibernian threw everything into attack.

The story of the night was Leeds' clever defence and the command performance given by Bremner.

It was not Revie's custom to mention individual players, but he made an exception this time, singling out Bremner for special mention, later citing the match as his finest in Leeds colours: 'It is not a thing I normally do, but Billy was absolutely superb. He gave one of the finest exhibitions I think I have ever seen from an individual player. He played a sweeper role and that was only the second time in his career that he has been in that position, yet he was unbelievably confident – just magic.'

Easter Road
Attendance: 36,051

Hibernian: McArthur, Bremner, Schaedler, Stanton, Black, Blackley, Edwards, Higgins (Hazel), Gordon, Cropley, Duncan

Leeds United: Shaw (Letheren), Reaney, Cherry, Bremner, Ellam, Yorath, Lorimer, Clarke, Jordan, Bates, F. Gray

43

Stoke City 3-2 Leeds United
First Division
23 February 1974

At the start of the campaign Don Revie had challenged his players to go through the League season unbeaten. By the end of February, what had once seemed a fanciful notion promised to become reality as the Whites continued to resist all comers.

By the time of their fixture with Stoke City on 23 February, United had played twenty-nine First Division games without seeing their colours lowered. If they could just avoid defeat at the Victoria Ground, a record established by Burnley in 1920/21 would be equalled.

At the time Stoke were sixteen places below Revie's men, but had themselves gone nine matches unbeaten.

The Leeds rearguard was forced to take the field without both Paul Reaney and Gordon McQueen, as had been the case a few days earlier when Second Division Bristol City put United out of the FA Cup. Terry Yorath and Roy Ellam deputised against Stoke, while Joe Jordan led the front line with Mick Jones injured. Otherwise, United's first choice line up was on duty, with Johnny Giles making his third successive start after returning from injuries sustained the previous October.

Most of the early exchanges were fought out in the middle third with both sides eager to contest possession and the challenges were not for the faint hearted.

United gained material reward for some early dominance when they broke the deadlock after fourteen minutes with a goal which provoked fierce protest from the home side.

City centre back Denis Smith brought Billy Bremner down just outside the Stoke penalty area. As the home defence readied themselves to defend the free-kick, the United captain seized the initiative. He caught Stoke on the hop, spotting the ball quickly and lobbing a shot directly into the unguarded net with goalkeeper Farmer barely making a move.

Referee John Homewood awarded the goal despite the angry remonstrations of the City players, who vigorously insisted that the kick had been taken too quickly.

Their rage was doubled four minutes later when United increased their advantage with a goal from Allan Clarke.

Johnny Giles manufactured the opening, lobbing the ball forward to Clarke, in space with only the goalkeeper to beat. The striker cushioned the pass with his thigh and swept the ball home, almost in the same movement.

It was the final act of the Irish schemer's afternoon, for he pulled his hamstring in the process and was forced to leave the field before play restarted.

United always prided themselves on being able to hang onto a lead, but on this occasion they were found wanting as Stoke launched a revival.

After twenty-seven minutes the Staffordshire outfit halved the arrears. Norman Hunter fouled John Mahoney just outside the United area and defender Mike Pejic stepped up to take the free-kick. He hammered in a fierce rising drive which flew past Harvey and inside the far post.

It was exactly what the home side required to get their teeth into the game and they stormed into a full-blooded assault on Harvey's area.

The momentum was almost exclusively with the Potters and by the thirty-fourth minute they were back on level terms. Ritchie headed the ball back from deep inside the United area to Hudson, who gave Harvey no chance with a shot from 12 yards.

Harvey's left foot and ankle were heavily strapped when the teams came back on for the second period. He was clearly struggling for mobility as a confident-looking City subjected his defence to a telling cross examination.

John Farmer could have hired a deckchair to watch the game in comfort such was the lack of action around his station. When Stoke took the lead, the only surprise was that it took them sixty-eight minutes to do so.

The goal came after a succession of corners had stoked up the pressure. Yorath's headed clearance to the third flag kick looped invitingly to the edge of the 6-yard box. Hurst nodded the ball back towards the far post and centre back Smith came hurtling through to head home powerfully.

The ecstatic home fans erupted gleefully, bating the opposition with chants of 'We want four, we want four.'

United did their best to rescue what looked a lost cause. Bremner and Madeley made ground on the right to give Lorimer the opportunity for a shot, though Farmer saved without difficulty. The Stoke goalkeeper was in action again moments later when he gathered a Jordan header, but Leeds never seemed to believe that they could get back on terms.

They did, though, show plenty of aggression. With six minutes to go, protests by Bremner and Clarke saw them booked for disputing the award of a goal kick. They were also involved in unseemly scuffles with Robertson and had a furious row with referee Homewood after the game.

All the passion failed to bring a single clear cut opportunity, and at the finish Leeds' proud record was left in tatters.

Paul Wilcox wrote in *The Guardian*: 'Leeds still managed some carefully moulded moves, mainly out of defensive positions, and Bremner was magnificent, scuttling around to curb Stoke's attacks and darting forward to try to restore that early vitality to attack.'

Publicly, Don Revie was magnanimous in defeat, but behind closed doors he was beside himself with anger. He made a point after the game of allowing the United players to overhear his conversation with Les Cocker. 'Time to get the chequebook out and sign some new players.' It was a customary tactic used by the manager to gee up his men, but this time it was born of genuine frustration.

On the back of the FA Cup shock at the hands of Bristol City, the defeat came as a real blow to United's confidence. It would be several weeks before they could rid themselves of the psychological impact, losing three further games in a matter of a few weeks. It came right in the end, but for the moment Leeds were tottering.

Victoria Ground
Attendance: 39,598

Stoke City: Farmer, Marsh, Pejic, Dodd, Smith, Mahoney, Robertson, Greenhoff, Hurst, Hudson, Ritchie

Leeds United: Harvey, Yorath, Cherry, Bremner, Ellam, Hunter, Lorimer, Clarke, Jordan, Giles (Cooper), Madeley

44

Leeds United 2-0 Derby County
First Division
6 April 1974

After months spent as overwhelming favourites to win the League title, United's form collapsed in February and March – a confident fighting force degenerated into a dispirited rabble.

A shock FA Cup exit at the hands of Bristol City preceded Stoke's destruction of a twenty-nine-game unbeaten League run; subsequently, Liverpool, Burnley and West Ham inflicted successive defeats to bring March to a miserable end. United's advantage over Liverpool shrank to four scant points, with the Merseysiders having three games in hand.

The Times' Tom German wrote: 'There must now be serious doubts whether Leeds United are capable of winning the Football League championship … It is sad to say of Leeds that they are looking more and more like an ordinary team, and that Bremner, still one of the finest players in Europe, is becoming increasingly like the captain, not perhaps of a sinking ship, but of one which has lost its way.'

United had six games left to rescue their season, though Liverpool's strong run of form had put them in the driving seat.

Old rivals Derby County offered Don Revie little in the way of respite. The Rams were no longer under the colourful management of Brian Clough, but new boss Dave Mackay had revived their fortunes. Derby's inspirational former skipper had presided over a run of two defeats in seventeen games, which left them third in the table.

If United were to regain the championship, it was essential that they rediscovered their scoring touch and they would have to do so in the absence of Mick Jones and Allan Clarke. Revie's solution was to deploy Billy Bremner alongside Joe Jordan, with Peter Lorimer recalled after being rested against West Ham.

Lorimer had been struggling, without a First Division goal from open play since his hat-trick against Birmingham in September, but he had a track record against Derby, having scored ten times in his previous ten appearances against them.

A crowd of almost 38,000 packed into Elland Road to see whether United could banish their jitters.

The first genuine opportunity came from a Derby free-kick on the edge of the Leeds area, and Harvey had to be alert to turn David Nish's long floating ball over his bar.

Referee John Williamson had a quiet word with Bremner after the United skipper sent Davies crashing to the turf. The incident was a sign of the home eleven's determination; they were desperate for the goal that would settle their nerves and they got it after seventeen minutes, the move a tribute to the quick thinking of Bremner and Lorimer.

Norman Hunter flighted a long ball for an unchallenged Joe Jordan to cleverly cushion a header sideways to Bremner, 35 yards out.

The Leeds captain had spotted a defensive gap and swept the ball on instantly with an inch-perfect chip. As it dropped just into the area, Lorimer, racing through the inside left channel, beat Rioch and, as Derby appealed for offside, clipped a cool left-footed lob over the advancing Boulton and just under the bar.

Recognising the importance of the goal, United players celebrated ecstatically, led by Lorimer.

There was no surrender from Derby, but United flourished as Giles, Madeley and Yorath exerted a midfield grip.

Jordan threatened twice, a fine Davies tackle being necessary when he bore down on goal and then a long ball from Yorath sent him speeding past Nish's attempted tackle, though the Scot spoilt his work by misfiring wildly.

When Bremner clashed in midfield with Scotland colleague Archie Gemmill, the referee awarded a free-kick to Derby but McQueen headed away in commanding style.

Bremner went close to increasing United's lead on the stroke of half-time, but they had to be satisfied with a single goal advantage at the break.

Derby were quickly onto the offensive when play restarted, but Harvey ended the threat, coming out quickly to dispossess Davies.

Around the hour, Hunter was left limping after a melee in the United goalmouth. He struggled on for a minute or two but then admitted defeat and slumped to the turf in obvious pain. After receiving treatment, he was able to play on but did so under handicap.

Rioch and Gemmill had gained a midfield foothold and Bourne, Davies and Hector threatened Harvey's goal as Derby strove to get on terms. Davies had United's defence in a tangle before the ball was scrambled away for a corner and Harvey showed excellent judgement when he darted to the edge of his penalty area to collect at the feet of Hector.

United, though, gave themselves breathing space after sixty-nine minutes when Bremner made it 2-0.

Cherry's free-kick from just inside the Derby half dropped invitingly to the edge of the box. Jordan could not get to it, but Nish's header was poor and Bremner, anticipating smartly, ran around the dropping ball and was in perfect position to slide coolly home from 15 yards. His accurate strike nestled smoothly into the corner of the net.

It was a masterly goal, and the gleeful United skipper lay there to receive the acclaim of his teammates.

Revie fed instructions to Yorath, demanding that United protect their advantage; there was to be no collapse, insisted Revie.

Derby sent on Alan Hinton as substitute for Rioch, almost gaining immediate rewards when Hinton's free-kick was headed just wide by Bourne. However, with McQueen and the limping Hunter oozing defiance, United ran down the clock to secure a much-needed victory, just their second since 9 February. The relief was palpable at the final whistle.

The gap at the top remained unchanged with Liverpool winning 2-1 at Anfield; the Reds had to come back from a goal down and needed a penalty and an own goal to do the trick against a QPR eleven that battled fiercely but to no avail. However, the victory against Derby revived what had started to seem a lost cause.

They were by no means home and dry and the next two games brought disappointing goalless draws. Nevertheless, the often nervy victory was a turning point, breathing new life into a faltering sprint to the finish. A trumpeting message of defiance had been sent across the Pennines to Liverpool.

Elland Road
Attendance: 37,838

Leeds United: Harvey, Reaney, Cherry, Bremner, McQueen, Hunter, Lorimer, Giles, Jordan, Yorath, Madeley

Derby County: Boulton, Webster, Nish, Rioch (Hinton), Daniel, Todd, Powell, Gemmill, Davies, Hector, Bourne

45

Leeds United 3-2 Ipswich Town
First Division
20 April 1974

As the championship race came down to the wire, long-term front runners Leeds were under the severest pressure from Liverpool.

On 9 February, the Whites' defeat of Manchester United at Old Trafford took them nine points clear with thirteen games left. But then an astonishing decline set in, with Leeds suffering four League defeats in the space of five weeks; their once-impregnable lead crumbled as Liverpool turned up the heat, winning match after match in an unbeaten run that stretched all the way back to Boxing Day when they had lost to Burnley.

West Ham's defeat of United on 30 March left Leeds with fifty-two points from thirty-six games; Liverpool had four points fewer, but three games in hand.

At that crucial moment, Don Revie's men managed to conjure a 2-0 defeat of Derby. When Liverpool's unbeaten run ended courtesy of a single goal at Sheffield United two days later, the advantage edged back towards Leeds.

In the following weeks, both teams fell victims to title jitters with a succession of draws, before they each registered a convincing victory on 16 April, Liverpool thrashing Manchester City 4-0 at Anfield and Leeds winning 2-0 at Sheffield United. Those results left the Whites four points clear with two games to play. Liverpool still had four fixtures remaining, but the Whites enjoyed a superior goal average.

20 April brought home fixtures for both clubs, United against third-placed Ipswich Town and Liverpool facing Merseyside rivals Everton. The bookmakers were clear about the destination of the title, quoting Leeds at odds of 9-2 on, while Liverpool were 7-2.

The Sheffield United game had saddled Leeds with a testing legacy; Jordan, McQueen, Clarke and Hunter were struggling to be ready, though Bremner, Jones, Yorath and Giles were considered likely to play.

In the end, McQueen, Clarke, Hunter, Bremner and Jones were all declared fit and there was a welcome boost with the return of long-term injury victim Eddie Gray, selected for the first time since September.

From the whistle, United came under severe pressure, but it was they who opened the scoring after sixteen minutes.

Brian Talbot's attempted one-two with Clive Woods was ended by a forceful McQueen intervention that found Lorimer down the right. Clarke and Jones were both waiting unmarked in the middle for a cross that never came, for Lorimer had eyes only for goal. He swerved a fiercely rising effort that flew past goalkeeper Cooper and into the net just inside the angle.

The goal gave United impetus and they showed renewed confidence and fluency as Billy Bremner drove them forward. Some direct running from Ipswich's front men threatened at the other end, but Leeds had the bit between their teeth and it was 2-0 after twenty-two minutes.

After Beattie nodded away a free-kick, Talbot was adjudged to have handled the dropping ball a few yards outside the Ipswich area. From the resultant free-kick Lorimer stepped up to crack in another tremendous drive. The keeper managed to block the effort, but when it ballooned up, the onrushing Bremner dived forward to nod the ball home.

There were subsequent Ipswich protests that Bremner was offside but the referee confirmed the goal.

That sparked a vigorous response from the visitors and they forced United onto defence, pulling a goal back five minutes later. Johnson picked the ball up in midfield to feed Mills on the left and the move continued with Woods in the inside left channel 30 yards from goal. An attempted one-two with Osborne foundered but the ball fell loose to Talbot, who fired home from near the penalty spot.

United would have preferred more than the 2-1 lead they had at the interval, and they were rocked when Ipswich drew level after fifty-four minutes.

Town midfielder Morris played the ball out to Woods, but his run was ended by a fearsome foot up challenge from Paul Reaney and Ipswich were awarded the free-kick. Morris fed Mills on the left and when Osborne fired in a shot cum cross, Hamilton flicked it past Harvey into the net.

Far from settling for a point, Bobby Robson's team pushed on but Leeds had come too far to pass up their opportunity and restored their lead after seventy minutes.

A period of United possession saw the ball fall to an advanced Reaney on the right and his looped cross was nodded on by Lorimer. The Scot was not a notable header of the ball but his flick was perfect and Clarke got onto the ball, controlled it well under pressure and hammered into the roof of the net from close range.

The defenders appealed fiercely that Clarke had handled the ball, but the referee ignored their protests and signalled the goal was good.

The home crowd roared United on as they looked for a fourth, but they were content to preserve their lead. Twelve minutes from time Clarke was booked for refusing to retreat 10 yards from an Ipswich free-kick and then the names of Bremner and Cherry followed into the official's notebook after dallying unnecessarily over a United free-kick.

The points were vital, made doubly valuable by the news from Anfield that Liverpool had been held to a goalless draw by Everton.

It was a breathtaking contest and United had been pressed sorely, but they had done the necessary. Don Revie was on the brink of regaining the League title he coveted so dearly, an outcome that was confirmed four days later without his men even needing to take the field when Liverpool lost at home to Arsenal.

Elland Road
Attendance: 44,015

Leeds United: Harvey, Reaney, Cherry, Bremner, McQueen, Hunter, Lorimer, Clarke, Jones, Madeley, E. Gray

Ipswich Town: Cooper, Burley, Mills, Morris, Hunter, Beattie, Hamilton, Talbot, Johnson, Osborne, Woods

46

Brazil 0-0 Scotland
World Cup Finals
18 June 1974

The Scotland squad that Billy Bremner led into the 1974 World Cup finals included four of his Leeds colleagues – David Harvey, Gordon McQueen, Peter Lorimer and Joe Jordan – with a fifth, Eddie Gray, omitted because of chronic injury problems.

As a fiercely patriotic Scot, Bremner was delighted, but came close to missing out on the opportunity after a pre-tournament incident in Norway.

Bremner and Celtic winger Jimmy Johnstone broke a curfew to attend a drinking session with sports writers in a student bar and led a sing-song. Scotland manager Willie Ormond arrived with a party in full voice and was enraged by what he saw; minutes later Dr Fitzsimmons, the Scottish FA's medical representative, led the two players away.

Bremner said:

I think everyone was waiting for the balloon to go up. It was one of those things. Neither of us could sleep because the rooms were so bad. We decided to go for a walk and bumped into the journalists ... We weren't out getting drunk or anything like that. We just couldn't rest. We explained this to the manager.

He was very good about it really because he could have gone off the deep end and sent us both back home. However, Willie Ormond was not one for locking up his players and, even though the press was having a field day with Jimmy and myself being nominated for public hanging when we got back home, he took a more lenient view.

Thus reprieved, Bremner led Scotland to a 2-0 victory over Zaire in their opening game. The Scots now faced holders Brazil, who had drawn 0-0 in their own first game with Yugoslavia. Bremner and his men gave a sterling performance, though the captain claimed,

We were over-cautious ... We paid them far too much respect for the first half before realising that they were human just like we were.

To be playing Brazil in the World Cup finals has to be every schoolboy's and man's dream. It certainly was mine. The travelling press pack typically had us well beaten before the game started, and that helped us to focus more on our strengths and put in a really determined showing. We didn't want to concede at all but we knew the early stages were important for us to defend as resolutely as we could.

The Brazil side was not a patch on the free-flowing team that had carried all before it four years earlier, and when the Scots came out of their shell, they rocked the South Americans and could easily have achieved an unexpected victory.

Referee Arie van Gamert allowed far too much latitude and the contest degenerated into a kicking match, with Jairzinho taking a wild swing at Joe Jordan and some equally robust retaliation.

Brazil still had plenty of gifted individuals and after thirteen minutes Wilson Piazza forced David Harvey into a great save, diving to turn aside a dipping shot. Levinha volleyed against the bar from the resulting flag kick.

After thirty-one minutes, Rivelino was cautioned for a wild tackle on Bremner; then Marinho sought to wind-up Joe Jordan, cuffing the striker around the head. Even when Luis Pereira blatantly body checked Peter Lorimer, it only brought a stern reprimand from the referee.

Such rough house tactics saw many of the neutrals in the stadium switch their affections to the Scots, though Bremner got into the act as the interval approached, taking out an opponent.

The second half saw Scotland raise their game, pushing hard for an opening goal with David Hay's shot from 30 yards turned over the bar by keeper Leao, who then saved Jordan's back-post header.

It was Bremner, though, who had the best opportunity from close in after Jordan's header from Lorimer's corner was only parried by Leao. It came so quickly that Bremner could only poke out a foot and the ball slipped agonisingly wide of the upright from 3 yards. Bremner held his head in in despair as the moment passed. He commented,

> We put a lot of pressure on the Brazilians and we were desperately close to scoring when the ball came off my shins and rebounded just inches the wrong side of the post when the goalkeeper was stranded. We were so very close but we just could not break them down ... I could not stop thinking about that nearly goal. We had been just two inches from a famous victory.
>
> It was a truly dreadful moment. I knew as soon as the ball came up to me it wasn't going to be easy for me to make a clean contact with it. It was spinning awkwardly and bounced, I tried to stab it home and got it all wrong. My heart was in my mouth and I honestly felt sick.

The game ended goalless and the South Americans capitalised by beating Zaire 3-0 in the final game. Yugoslavia had put nine past the Africans and a 1-1 draw with Scotland was enough for them to head the group with all three sides tied on four points and the Scots travelling home early, undefeated but desperately disappointed.

Waldstadion, Frankfurt
Attendance: 62,000

Scotland: Harvey, Jardine, McGrain, Bremner, Holton, Buchan, Morgan, Hay, Jordan, Dalglish, Lorimer

Brazil: Leao, Mario Marinho, Nelinho, Luis Pereira, Chagas, Eiveline, Paulo Cesar Lima, Wilson da Silva Piazza, Jairzinho, Leivinha (Paulo Cesar Carpegiani), Mirandinha

47

Liverpool 1-1 Leeds United
FA Charity Shield
10 August 1974

The 1974 Charity Shield match, staged for the first time at Wembley, was both the final game in charge of Liverpool for Bill Shankly and the debut at the helm of the Elland Road club for Brian Clough. When Don Revie had departed to take over the England team in the summer, the Leeds Board had shocked the footballing world by replacing him with one of the club's fiercest critics.

Leeds and Liverpool had fought some bitter battles down the years, but it is doubtful whether there was ever an angrier encounter than there was that day.

There were niggling fouls from the off with Billy Bremner and Johnny Giles nipping at the heels of the Liverpool players. The arrival of the abrasive Clough had disturbed the United camp and they were in no mood to contribute to a frivolous showpiece event.

Early in the game, a Liverpool player pressed Giles from behind and clipped his ankle – the Irishman was never one to take such treatment lying down and lashed out at the offender. He got a booking and a stiff lecture for his trouble.

That was only the precursor to the main event of the afternoon as the mood became fractious. It was six of one and half-a-dozen of the other, but Clough, with his customary black and white vision, was clear about who he felt was the guilty party in the clash just after the hour which remains the lasting memory of the game: 'Billy Bremner's behaviour was scandalous, producing one of the most notorious incidents in Wembley history. It was as if the players were offering grounds for all my criticism that they had resented so much.

'Bremner seemed intent on making Kevin Keegan's afternoon an absolute misery. He kicked him just about everywhere ... until it became only a matter of time before a confrontation exploded. There is only so much any man can take. Eventually, inevitably, Keegan snapped – and they were both sent off, Keegan whipping off his shirt and flinging it to the ground as he went. It was a stupid gesture, but I could understand the man's anger and frustration. It was the action of a player who felt he had been wronged, not only by an opponent but by a referee who had failed to stamp out intimidation before it reached the stage of retaliation. Keegan will have regretted his touchline tantrum immediately.

'Keegan was an innocent party who had been pushed beyond the limit by an opponent who appeared determined to eliminate him from the match, one way or another. I told Bremner afterwards that he had been responsible for the confrontation.'

The offence resulted in a lengthy ban for both men and it was October before Bremner played again, by which time Clough's ill-fated period at Leeds had ended.

The game itself was a thoroughly ill-tempered affair with good football in short supply. With the players too busy kicking each other to notice, the match petered to a 1-1 stalemate. Leeds had been chasing the game since Phil Boersma opened the scoring in the twentieth minute and finally drew level when Trevor Cherry headed home after seventy minutes. The goals were just a distracting sideshow to the violence.

The game went to penalties and, with the scores balanced precariously at 5-5 in sudden death, Leeds bizarrely chose keeper David Harvey to go next. Harvey duly obliged by thumping the ball over the bar. Ian Callaghan smashed home the winner for Liverpool, but the match will be remembered only for Keegan and Bremner's bare-chested outrage.

There were some hysterical newspaper articles over the next few days and some of the holier-than-thou members of the media were all for kicking both clubs out of the First Division. As it was, Keegan and Bremner were banned for eleven matches in all and fined £500 apiece, but no further action was taken.

Jonathan Wilson wrote in *Brian Clough – The Biography: Nobody Ever Says Thank You*:

> Later that week came the disciplinary hearing ... Oddly, Clough didn't speak on Bremner's behalf, instead handing that responsibility to Maurice Lindley, which hardly suggested a manager backing his captain to the hilt.
>
> The hearing suspended Bremner until the end of September and imposed a £500 fine which Clough insisted Bremner pay out of his own pocket. Bremner pointed out that Revie had always made sure the club paid the players' fines, to which Clough replied, 'Don's not here any more.' Jimmy Gordon witnessed the exchange and realised from the look on Bremner's face that Clough had no chance.
>
> Yet Clough went out of his way to get Bremner onside. As the captain served his suspension, Clough made a point of including him in team talks, sat next to him on the coach, and asked him to act as assistant manager at a reserve game to report back on the form of McKenzie and Jordan. Bremner refused, citing a prior engagement.

The fiasco was a low point in the history of United. The incident and the appalling relationship with the new manager destabilised the club and Leeds made an awful start to their defence of the League. They were nineteenth after winning just four points from their first six games, form that cost Clough his job and Leeds the title in a season when Derby County won through with one of the lowest point totals ever.

Wembley Stadium
Attendance: 67,000

Leeds United: Harvey; Reaney, McQueen, Hunter, Cherry; Lorimer, Bremner, Giles, E Gray; Clarke (McKenzie), Jordan

Liverpool: Clemence; Smith, Thompson, Hughes, Lindsay; Heighway, Cormack, Hall, Callaghan; Keegan, Boersma

48

Leeds United 2-1 Barcelona
European Cup Semi-Final, First Leg
9 April 1975

After the removal of Brian Clough, Billy Bremner's relationship with Johnny Giles grew fraught, as recalled by the Irishman:

On the night that Brian Clough was sacked, Norman Hunter was at the club, having a meeting about his testimonial, when he met Manny Cussins. He was told by Manny that the Board was about to offer me the manager's job.

But Manny didn't call that Thursday night. Instead he phoned at seven o'clock the following morning. He wasn't the most articulate of men at the best of times, so when he came on the line, he said without any preamble, 'I say I say I say, will you take the job?'

I told him I couldn't give him an answer there and then, that there was a lot to talk about before I could make that decision. We agreed to meet at the ground at nine o'clock.

And there was a lot to talk about too. This was my first contact with any of the Board since they had rejected Don's suggestion that I should be offered the manager's job, and I wasn't too pleased about that. Clearly, there would have been a presumption on their part that I was keen to get such a prestigious position, but I had mixed feelings about it. I certainly had ambitions to go into management when I finished playing – but I also really wanted to continue playing. I knew that if I took the job, I could not be a player-manager at a major club like Leeds.

I hadn't become the sort of hardened old pro who had lost touch with the magic of playing. Even at the age of thirty-three, I was hanging on to the dream. For me, football always came back to that. So I had to decide ... if it was worth missing out on two or three years of playing, to take on one of the biggest managerial jobs in England. I was still wrestling with this as I drove into the ground. And when I passed the treatment room to go upstairs to the boardroom, I bumped into Billy Brenner.

'I knew he was having treatment for a calf injury but I was still a bit surprised to see him at the club so early. I was on my way up the stairs when he joined me.

'I told them that if they didn't offer you the job, I was going to apply for it,' he said. I was preoccupied about the meeting, so what Billy said didn't really register with me. Sure enough, Manny and the directors were assembled in his office, but as soon as I sat down he surprised me, 'Look, what we want John, is for you to continue just being a player,' he said.

'Hang on,' I said. 'I already am a player. You rang me at seven o'clock this morning to ask me if I would take the manager's job. Now you're telling me you want me to continue as a player. So what is this all about?'

Then, it started to get ridiculous. He told me that they wanted me and Syd Owen and Billy to take the team for this Saturday. I told him there was no way I would do that. Then Manny started waffling about things happening. Nothing he said was coherent or made much sense to me, but one thing was clear — I was no longer being offered the job that I'd already been offered a couple of hours ago.

Soon I was back in the car driving home. I was still befuddled by it all. Then, I started to rerun that conversation I'd had with Billy. But it still didn't dawn on me ... And then the pieces started to drift together. Suddenly it hit me, as it should have done earlier: Billy ... had ... applied for ... the ... job.

In my mind, which wasn't really focused on what he was telling me, I was still assuming that Billy was saying he'd apply for the job in certain circumstances. But it transpired that after the chairman had phoned me at home, a club employee, who was friendly with Billy, had told him about my meeting in the boardroom at nine. That's why Billy was at the ground when I arrived. Billy had been to see the directors and had applied for the job while I was on the way in. Which explained the Board's change of heart between seven and nine o'clock. And I could now see their dilemma. Billy's application had effectively scuppered things as far as I was concerned, because it would split the dressing room. Now, they couldn't offer the position to either of us.

I would have had no objection to Billy applying for the job, but it had never entered my head that he was interested. I was thirty-three and felt it might be premature to give up playing, but Billy was only thirty-one.

We were due back at the ground at one o'clock that day for training and, before I arrived, the other players asked Billy to confirm that he had applied for the job. When he said that he had, he got an icy response. Billy decided not to travel with the team for the next game.

I was amazed at him. Had I known of his interest in the job, I would have withdrawn any interest of my own. I can only imagine his reasons for doing what he did. He was close to Don, and it's possible he might have been hurt by Don's recommendation of me as manager, rather than him. Maybe he felt it undermined him in some way, the public face of Leeds.

This sad situation lasted for a short while, until Billy withdrew his application, but by then, the Board was already seeking alternatives.

The directors invited Bolton boss Jimmy Armfield, formerly captain of Blackpool and England, to steady the ship. He did a good job in that respect, smoothing the feathers that Clough had ruffled, and reviving the family atmosphere on which the club thrived. That included arranging for the club to stage a version of *Cinderella* over Christmas, with Bremner playing Buttons, Norman Hunter as Prince Charming, Duncan McKenzie in the title role and the Gray brothers as the ugly sisters.

Armfield said later of Bremner:

The team were struggling, they had lost Don Revie in the summer and had gone through a traumatic 44 days with his successor, Brian Clough. When I arrived, Billy was injured and the team was near the bottom with six points from nine matches. One day I was chatting to Bob English, our kit man, and he said: 'Don't worry, you'll see a difference when Billy's back. When Billy plays, they all play.' And he was right. We never looked back once Billy was fit again. He was a real firebrand but people forget what a gifted player he was. Good touch on the ball, very clever, with just about the best reverse pass I ever saw. He was a great competitor, too, with a tremendous amount of pride. He wanted the job after Clough left and I suspect there was a bit of resentment when I arrived. I didn't go out of my way to win him over. I just treated him with the respect he deserved and we became close.

Armfield improved onfield fortunes and the Whites recovered sufficiently to earn a mouth-watering European Cup semi-final pairing with Barcelona, led by Dutch superstars Johan Cruyff and Johan Neeskens.

Leeds saw off FC Zurich, Ujpest Dozsa and Anderlecht on the way through to the last four and went into the tie in good heart, though a run of five points from seven games had seen their League ranking fall from sixth to tenth. They had also gone out of the FA Cup after a four-game marathon quarter-final against Ipswich.

The side that Bremner led out for the first leg against Barca at Elland Road was an interesting selection, with Armfield selecting Paul Madeley and Terry Yorath at the expense of Norman Hunter and Peter Lorimer. The tactical switch was designed to neutralise the threat of Cruyff and give Leeds added steel in midfield.

Armfield saw his men begin the game in dominating fashion and it was Bremner who gave them the best possible start when he became the first player to score against Barcelona in the competition when he struck after nine minutes.

The skipper had started the game in an advanced role and had already gone close to playing Clarke in on goal with a good ball into the area, but the England striker was penalised for a foul on the keeper.

Bremer was on hand to profit when Giles lofted a long ball to Joe Jordan around the edge of the penalty area. As the striker's clever header dropped perfectly into space in the right channel, Bremner was on it in a trice, leaving his marker standing to settle on the ball and power it stylishly past Barca keeper Sadurni.

Bremner had a happy knack of coming up trumps in semi-finals for Leeds and there was no mistaking his joy as he did the trick again.

With the second leg to come in the unwelcoming Nou Camp Stadium, United could not be content with a one-goal advantage and continued to press, with both Allan Clarke and Gordon McQueen going close with headers and Joe Jordan's shot testing Sadurni, but a second score seemed beyond them.

A class act like Cruyff always presented a danger, however, and though Paul Madeley nullified much of his threat, United knew they had to remain alert.

After a United corner in the sixty-sixth minute, Cruyff broke away against a stranded Leeds defence and things looked ominous until Paul Reaney dispossessed Heredia on the edge of the Leeds area. He was unfortunate to be penalised but it gave Barca a decent opportunity. Cruyff stood over the free-kick, before slipping it to Juan Manuel Asensi, who fired home.

United kept going and regained the lead with twelve minutes remaining. Madeley took the ball forward purposely before feeding an overlapping Reaney down the right. The full-back sent over a perfect cross for Jordan. Yorath attempted in vain to get onto the Scot's header but it fell perfectly for Clarke, who drove home without hesitation to send the crowd into glorious celebration.

The 2-1 win left Barca happy with the away goal and confident that they could seal the tie in Spain, though Bremner confidently claimed, 'A one-goal lead is enough because we expect to win over there. I was not impressed by Barcelona at all. We tend to build up these continental teams too much and when the game is played, they don't turn out the way we feared.'

Elland Road
Attendance: 50,393

Leeds United: Stewart, Reaney, F. Gray, Bremner, McQueen, Madeley, Yorath, Clarke, Jordan, Giles, E. Gray

Barcelona: Sadurni, Costas (Rife), Marinho, Gallego, De La Cruz, Neeskens (Juan Carlos), Rexach, Migueli, Cruyff, Asensi, Heredi

49

Barcelona 1-1 Leeds United
European Cup Semi-Final, Second Leg
23 April 1975

Leeds United were seasoned European campaigners and had made a habit of outstanding away performances during their ten seasons of competition. The prospect of meeting mighty Barcelona in their awesome Nou Camp took things to a whole new level, and United were generally rated as outsiders to reach the final, though they were confident in their ability to do the necessary.

Joe Jordan, outstanding in the first leg at Elland Road, was in supreme form again in Spain, winning everything in the air, as recalled by Peter Lorimer:

> We were seven minutes into our European Cup semi-final return meeting with Barcelona when keeper David Stewart hoisted a clearance deep into the opposition half. As the ball dropped, big Joe Jordan rose high above his marker and flicked it into my path, 20 yards or so from goal on the right-hand side. A couple of paces and bang. I just let one go and what a feeling to see it fly into the top corner.
>
> It was a huge relief, as well, because it meant we had an all-important away goal. Barcelona had to score twice, just to take it to extra time, and that wasn't going to happen. No-one got two goals back on Leeds United in those days.

Manager Jimmy Armfield claimed that the goal was down to tactics:

> They used man to man marking very rigidly, and so we used a tactic that, to be honest, I was surprised they fell for. We started with Peter Lorimer on the left side of midfield, and of course he was picked up by a right-footed player who stuck to him.
>
> After 15 minutes I told Peter to switch to the right side, and sure enough, his marker went with him. A few minutes later Joe Jordan got a flick on and Peter latched on to it and ran at his marker.
>
> As he came towards goal he switched it on to his right foot, which wrongfooted his marker and gave him the space to get in a shot – and being Lorimer, he hit it beautifully.

The goal was Lorimer's thirtieth in Europe, a British record at the time, and meant that the Spaniards would now need to score three times to oust Leeds, a vital advantage.

Barca had gone close early on with a header from Heredia but the goal gave them food for thought. They were soon piling forward towards David Stewart's goal but United stood up well to the pressure.

Bremner was in the wars in a hard-fought midfield battle with Cruyff and Neeskens, though Terry Yorath's steely determination offered some defensive assurance in the middle of the park.

In the second half, the Leeds captain was penalised for a strong tackle on the edge of his area shortly after being laid low at the other end by a fierce Barca challenge. It had looked a clean challenge and Bremner was distraught when the free-kick was awarded, but it came to nothing. However, after sixty-nine minutes, Manuel Clares headed home the cross from Francisco Gallego to bring Barcelona level on the night.

It was clear that it would need to be all hands to the pump over the final twenty minutes and the challenge became even fiercer a few minutes later when young Gordon McQueen lost his rag and was dismissed from the field when he punched Clares.

United were now penned deep into their own half as 110,000 fanatical Spanish supporters urged the Catalans on. Billy Bremner was everywhere as Leeds manfully defied everything Barca could throw at them. Ten years of battle campaign had given them a steely backbone and Bremner and his men were admirable in their work as they denied Barca the goal that would have drawn them level on aggregate. In the final minute, Bremner combined with keeper Stewart to shepherd a header from Neeskens off the United goal line.

At the end, it was job very well done as a justifiably proud captain basked in the glory of reaching the European Cup final for the first time, sinking to his knees in joy with arms aloft in triumph.

Jimmy Armfield said,

> I can remember the game in Barcelona very well; you don't ever quite forget the details of a match as big as that.
>
> We had the experience and the fact is we were the better side. In fact, we were the best team in Europe, no question. When we went back to the hotel the players didn't want to go out, but they had a quiet celebration of their own; they were proud of what they'd achieved, and they had a right to be.

Nou Camp
Attendance: 110,000

Barcelona: Sadurni, Marinho, Gallego, Bianqueti, De La Cruz, Neeskens, Rexach, Heredia, Cruyff, Asensi (Rife), Clares

Leeds United: Stewart, Cherry, F. Gray, Bremner, McQueen, Hunter, Lorimer, Clarke, Jordan, Yorath, Madeley

50

Bayern Munich 2-0 Leeds United
European Cup Final
28 May 1975

When Billy Bremner led Leeds out for the European Cup final against Bayern Munich in the Parc des Princes Stadium in Paris on 28 May 1975, it should have been the crowning point of the most successful period in the club's history, but the events that followed that evening led the Leeds captain to describe the event as 'the most disappointing moment of my soccer career'.

United could have been forgiven for thinking that they had already done the hard part by seeing off Barcelona in the semi-finals; Bayern Munich were considered less of a challenge after finishing tenth in the Bundesliga, despite being holders of the trophy and fielding five members of the West Germany side that had lifted the World Cup the previous summer.

Leeds would highlight the disgraceful refereeing display of Michel Kitabdjian as the key reason for their failure to beat Bayern, but the Germans were up in arms in the opening minutes when the match official declined to caution Terry Yorath. The Welsh international had taken out Bjorn Andersson, leading to the Swedish international being replaced by Josef Weiss.

The moment encapsulated United's determination; they dominated the opening half, forcing Bayern into a rearguard action that saw them fortunate to survive two concerted appeals for penalties, with skipper Franz Beckenbauer at the heart of both incidents.

He appeared to handle the ball from a grounded position as Peter Lorimer attempted to take the ball past him, and then brought Allan Clarke crashing to the ground minutes before the interval.

The previous incident had been disappointing for United but the German's scything foul on Clarke was nowhere near the ball and left United apoplectic.

Leeds kept their heads and continued to boss matters, with Bremner and Johnny Giles controlling the midfield. The Whites came close on several occasions, benefiting from the aerial dominance of Joe Jordan, and they profited from balls to his head. Sepp Maier denied them time and again and when Jordan found a way past the Bayern defence to fire in right-footed, the keeper held the ball in impressive fashion.

After an hour Bremner looked likely to open the scoring but Maier denied him from close range after he got on to Madeley's header.

In the sixty-sixth minute, it seemed that Leeds had finally opened the scoring when Lorimer volleyed powerfully into the net after Bayern had failed to clear a free-kick from Giles. Bremner was off celebrating with the others but the referee chose to disallow the effort for the United captain being in an offside position. Kitabdjian had originally awarded the goal, but had been persuaded by Beckenbauer to consult the linesman.

Bremner commented,

We began the second half like the first, attacking all the time. I knew that by pushing forward so much we were leaving ourselves a little vulnerable at the back. But I thought the risk of a counter attack was worth it because we were so much on top.

Leeds were pulverising them until the second turning point in the game.

A Peter Lorimer free-kick was flicked on by the head of Paul Madeley to me in an unmarked position in the penalty area. I shot from close-range, but Sepp Maier saved well.

A goal then could have made all the difference, to the result and the scenes afterwards.

Moments later ... a thunderbolt shot from Peter Lorimer crashed into the net. I leaped into the air. It was all over, I thought. That was the big breakthrough we wanted ... the European Cup was ours.

But no ... the referee disallowed the goal. At the time, I couldn't see anything wrong. I was furious, so were my teammates. Afterwards I was told television pictures revealed I was fractionally offside.

What made it so annoying at the time was the ref's indecision. First he pointed to the centre circle, then changed his mind. No one knew what was going on. Five minutes or so later Bayern took the lead. They broke quickly and midfielder Franz Roth slipped a Paul Madeley tackle to score.

The black mood of the United supporters was not helped when Roth's well-placed effort into the corner beat goalkeeper David Stewart.

United might yet have come back from that effort as Eddie Gray came on for Yorath in the seventy-ninth minute to lead a response, but within two minutes Bayern were two goals ahead and the United resolve was crushed.

Gerd Muller made his only contribution of the night when he got ahead of Madeley and first to Kapellman's cross from the right to turn the ball home from close range.

A United supporter attempted to invade the pitch and was badly beaten by baton-wielding police. His fellow fans reacted angrily, tearing up seats and throwing them angrily down onto the playing area.

The United players were so dejected after the game that they consigned their runners-up medals to the dressing room table as they left for the coach back to their hotel.

Billy Bremner said,

What made defeat so hard to take was the fact Leeds had dominated the game, did 90 per cent of the attacking, had what at first looked a good goal disallowed and were refused one of the most blatant penalties I've ever seen.

Bayern only had two shots at goal, but they were enough to give them the trophy for the second year in succession.

The defeat was made even harder to bear by the appalling behaviour of a handful of our supporters who went berserk in the stadium and caused so much damage and terror as they ran amok in the streets of Paris after the match.

A lot of them may not realise their behaviour contributed to our defeat! When play was stopped because of all the missiles that were being thrown from behind the goal, we lost some of our composure. We had been playing well up to then, but once the game got going again we couldn't recapture the same rhythm.

I'm not saying that incident would have altered the result, but it might have done.

The majority of our supporters were tremendous and were as disgusted as everyone by the actions of the minority. I saw some of those genuine fans afterwards. They were crying and ashamed.

At that meeting afterwards I was criticised by those officials and Pressmen for leading the Leeds team to applaud the fans. They completely misinterpreted my action. I assumed all the troublemakers had either been thrown out or had left the stadium early, and only genuine fans remained.

We'd played our hearts out, but failed to turn our superiority into goals. For almost the entire first half we had attacked and tried to penetrate Bayern's eight-man defence. We created so many chances, but just could not score.

It was a desperately disappointing finale to what had been a momentous period in the history of Leeds United, undeniably spelling the end of their dominance of the British and European game. Bremner had been captain through virtually all that time, personifying the clenched-fist determination of the club, unwanted outsiders who shook up the First Division and ushered in an era of professionalism and gamesmanship. They were unloved by many but acknowledged by all as fearsome opponents. The shame was that United never converted their dominance into the silverware that it merited, but Bremner was outstanding in his leadership of and contributions to their vainglorious pursuits of glory.

Parc des Princes
Attendance: 48,374

Bayern Munich: Maier, Durnberger, Andersson (Weiss), Schwarzenbeck, Beckenbauer, Roth, Tortensson, Zobel, Muller, Hoeness (Wunder), Kapellmann

Leeds United: Stewart, Reaney, F. Gray, Bremner, Madeley, Hunter, Lorimer, Clarke, Jordan, Giles, Yorath (E. Gray)

Epilogue

The side that Don Revie had so assiduously assembled was dismantled by Jimmy Armfield in the years following the European Cup final defeat to Bayern. In September 1976, Billy Bremner, aged thirty-three, set aside all thoughts of eking his playing days out at Leeds, instead accepting an offer from Second Division Hull City, though saying goodbye was no easy matter.

Bremner: 'After I had signed the contract I was all smiles, but inside I felt numb. There was a lump in my throat and I felt near to tears. It all seemed so unreal. All my footballing life I had been at Elland Road and yet here I was leaving the place ... I was leaving home.'

Two years later, Bremner was appointed manager of Doncaster Rovers, then struggling in Division Four, and led them to promotion in 1981. Donny were relegated in 1983 but returned to the Third Division at the first attempt.

When the Leeds United directors sacked Eddie Gray in 1985, they turned to Bremner in an attempt to revive the club's fortunes.

Bremner said,

Being manager of the club was totally different from before. Leeds was still a very big club with tremendous support, but there was a lot of work to be done. It was great to be back at Elland Road where everything was so familiar to me. At times, I almost expected Don Revie to walk in and tell me to get out of his chair. Yet, somehow, the place seemed run down and I knew that the only way to build it up again was to get the right results on the park as quickly as possible.

Bremner steered the club clear of relegation and then sparked a revival during a memorable 1986/87 campaign. They reached the last four of the FA Cup where they lost 3-2 to eventual winners Coventry City after extra time in a clash widely claimed to be one of the greatest ever semi-finals. Their late run also took Leeds into the first end of season play-offs but they had to give way to Charlton in a replayed final. Midfielder John Sheridan looked to have won the game for Bremner's men but Peter Shirtliff scored twice in the closing moments to deny them.

Bremner's reward for the near misses was a contract extension with United, installed as promotion favourites. They failed to live up to expectations, finishing seventh, and a poor start to the 1988/89 season saw Bremner sacked.

Bremner:

There was a big crowd of fans. I didn't know what to expect. I could understand them being angry about the lack of success, they felt exactly as I did myself. They closed in on me and then held out their hands for me to shake. They were marvellous and they gave me a real lift. I could take the sack but I didn't want to lose the affection of the fans. I thought the world of them and I hope that they felt the same way about me.

The Scot returned to Doncaster the following July but could not work his magic a second time and he resigned in November 1991 with Rovers sitting at the bottom of the Fourth Division, while his beloved Leeds were on their way to a totally unexpected League title triumph under the leadership of his successor, Howard Wilkinson.

Bremner would never work in football again.

Bibliography

Bagchi, Rob, and Rogerson, Paul, *The Unforgiven: The Story of Don Revie's Leeds United* (Aurum Press, 2009).

Bale, Bernard, *Bremner! The Legend of Billy Bremner* (Andre Deutsch, 1999).

Black, Jim, *Jinky – The Biography of Jimmy Johnstone* (Sphere, 2010).

Bremner, Billy, *You Get Nowt For Being Second* (Souvenir Press, 1969).

Broadbent, Rick, *Looking For Eric: In Search of the Leeds Greats* (Mainstream Publishing, 2002).

Charlton, Jack, *Jack Charlton: The Autobiography* (Corgi Books, 1997).

Giles, Johnny, *John Giles: A Football Man – The Autobiography* (Hodder, 2011).

Gray, Eddie, *Marching on Together: My Life at Leeds United* (Hodder & Stoughton, 2001).

Harrison, Paul, *Billy Bremner: Keep Fighting – The Definitive Biography* (Black and White Publishing, 2010).

Hermiston, Roger, *Clough and Revie: The Rivals Who Changed the Face of English Football* (Mainstream Publishing, 2011).

Hunter, Norman, *Biting Talk: My Autobiography* (Hodder & Stoughton, 2004).

Jarred, Martin, and Macdonald, Malcolm, *Leeds United: The Complete Record* (DB Publishing, 2012).

Jordan, Joe, with Lawton, James, *Behind the Dream: My Autobiography* (Hodder & Stoughton 2004).

Lorimer, Peter, *Peter Lorimer: Leeds and Scotland Hero* (Mainstream Publishing, 2002).

Lennox, Bobby, *Thirty Miles from Paradise: My Story* (Headline, 2008).

Mourant, Andrew, *Don Revie: Portrait of a Footballing Enigma* (Mainstream Publishing, 2003).

Saffer, David, *Sniffer: The Life and Times of Allan Clarke* (NPI Media Group, 2001).

Sprake, Stuart, *Careless Hands: Gary Sprake Biography: The Forgotten Truth of Gary Sprake* (The History Press, 2006).

Sutcliffe, Richard, *Bremner: The Complete Biography* (Great Northern Books, 2011).

Sutcliffe, Richard, *Revie Revered and Reviled* (Great Northern Books, 2010).

Tomas, Jason, *The Leeds United Story* (Littlehampton Book Services, 1971).

Wilson, Jonathan, *Brian Clough – The Biography: Nobody Ever Says Thank You* (Orion, 2012).